MILITARY LAW HANDBOOK FOR COMMANDERS

MILITARY LAW HANDBOOK FOR COMMANDERS

Second Edition

Maj. Gen. NILENDRA KUMAR AVSM, VSM

Director, Amity Law School, Noida

Former Judge Advocate General (Army)

Universal

Law Publishing Co. Pvt. Ltd.

NEW DELHI - INDIA

First Edition 2001
Second Edition 2011

ISBN : 978-93-5035-026-3

Published by
UNIVERSAL LAW PUBLISHING CO. PVT. LTD.
C-FF-1A, Dilkhush Industrial Estate,
(Near Azadpur Metro Station) G.T. Karnal Road,
Delhi-110 033
Tel : 011-27438103, 27215334, 42381334
Fax : 011-27458529
E-mail *(For sales inquiries)* : sales@unilawbooks.com
E-mail *(For editorial inquiries)* : edit@unilawbooks.com
Website : www.unilawbooks.com

Recommended citation: *Military Law Handbook for Commanders,* Maj Gen Nilendra Kumar, 2nd Edn. (New Delhi: Universal Law Publishing Co. Pvt. Ltd., 2011)

Computer Typeset at Aesthetic & *Printed* at Mudrak, New Delhi

This book is dedicated to all the formation commanders who shoulder the responsibility for the defence of our country.

PREFACE TO THE SECOND EDITION

The new edition of the book has taken into account a number of new changes. Setting up of the Armed Forces Tribunal has added an entirely new dimension to military discipline dispensation and service conditions governance. The Right to Information Act is now in place and makes commanders and designated officers responsible for supply of information. Adoption of Information Technology has imposed its own mandate on the armed forces. Environmental considerations have come to play a significant role. Human Rights regime carries its own non-derogable expectations. Women officers are now posted to the Regiments and Corps in greater numbers. This edition has taken a stock of such a situation and emerged as a knowledge kit for the units and formations.

Any comments or suggestions would be invaluable for further improvements in its contents and approach.

NOIDA

February, 2011 **Maj. Gen. Nilendra Kumar**

ले. जनरल पंकज जोशी, पी.वी.एस.एम., ए.वी.एस.एम., वी.एस.एम.,
जनरल आफिस कमाडिंग-इन-चीफ
Lt Gen PS Joshi, PVSM, AVSM, VSM
General Officer Commanding-in-Chief

मुख्यालय मध्य कमान, लखनऊ - २२६००२
Headquarter Central Command, Lucknow - 226002

FOREWORD TO THE FIRST EDITION

Legal awareness and proper adherence to the prevailing Code has come to acquire increasing importance for the commanders at all levels. Specific provisions meant for due compliance and guidelines for the benefit of commanders exist in the shape of statutory sections, rules, regulations, Army orders, instructions and policy letters issued from time to time by various authorities. However, non availability of suitable reference material is a major handicap to the formation commanders.

Brig Nilendra Kumar has drawn upon his long experience with the JAG's Dept to collate relevant information in this regard. In the process he has accomplished a commendable task to produce a hand book for use by the commanders and staff officers entrusted with handling disciplinary cases having a legal bearing.

I am confident that the painstaking efforts made by the author would be of practical use to the commanders and others in correct and timely disposal of such cases. I wish his efforts all success.

7th April, 2001

PS JOSHI
Lt Gen

PREFACE TO THE FIRST EDITION

While the primary task for the commanders would continue to demand a focus on the defence preparedness and war efforts, a high state of discipline will be a prerequisite in that regard. Sound administration and personnel management calls for due emphasis on fair play, adherence to the laid down norms and human treatment of the subordinates.

An attempt has been made in this book to compile and catalogue the powers available to the formation commanders in connection with various aspects having legal bearings to enable them to apply their mind for fair and correct action as regards offenders and others concerned.

It is hoped the work would serve as a ready reckoner for the commanders to enable them to discharge their duties effectively.

Lucknow

4th April, 2001 **Author**

CONTENTS

PART I

DISCIPLINE, VIGILANCE, COMPLAINTS, PETITIONS AND APPEALS, MAINTENANCE, DEFENCE OF COURT CASES, HUMAN RIGHTS AND ARBITRATION

PART II

POWERS OF FORMATION COMMANDERS

PART III

THE ARMY ACT, 1950

CHAPTER I

PRELIMINARY

CHAPTER II

SPECIAL PROVISIONS FOR THE APPLICATION OF ACT IN CERTAIN CASES

CHAPTER III

COMMISSION, APPOINTMENT AND ENROLMENT

CHAPTER VII

PUNISHMENTS

CHAPTER VIII

PENAL DEDUCTIONS

Sections Page

CHAPTER IX

ARREST AND PROCEEDINGS BEFORE TRIAL

CHAPTER X

COURTS-MARTIAL

CHAPTER XI

PROCEDURE OF COURTS-MARTIAL

Sections Page

ABBREVIATIONS USED

AA	-	Army Act
AG	–	Adjutant General
AHQ	–	Army Headquarters
AI	–	Army Instruction
AO	–	Army Order
AR	–	Army Rule/Assam Rifles
AWWA	–	Army Wives Welfare Association
accn	–	Accommodation
allce	–	Allowance
Art	–	Article
att	–	Attached
auth	–	Authority
bde	–	Brigade
CBI	–	Central Bureau of Investigation
CDA	–	Controller of Defence Accounts
CM	–	Court Martial
CO	–	Commanding Officer
C of I	–	Court of Inquiry
COS	–	Chief of Staff
COAS	–	Chief of the Army Staff
CVC	–	Central Vigilance Commission
cdr	–	Commander
civ	–	Civilian
DCM	–	District Court Martial
DDE	–	Dept of Defence Estates
DSR	–	Defence Services Regulations
DV	–	Discipline & Vigilance
Docu	–	Document
Fd	–	Field
fmn	–	Formation
GCM	–	General Court Martial
GOI	–	Government of India
indep	–	Independent

info	–	information
JAG	–	Judge Advocate General
LPA	–	Letter Patent Appeal
MACT	–	Motor Accident Claims Tribunal
MES	–	Military Engineering Service
MML	–	Manual of Military Law
MNS	–	Military Nursing Service
MOD	–	Ministry of Defence
MS	–	Military Secretary
MT	–	Mechanical Transport
Maint	–	Maintenance
NHRC	–	National Human Rights Commission
OIC	–	Officer-in-charge
PBOR	–	Personnel below officer rank
PCP	–	Post Confirmation Petition
POW	–	Prisoners of War
pdgs	–	Proceedings
Pers	–	Personnel
Pt	–	Point
RA	–	Regulations for the Army
RI	–	Rigorous Imprisonment
Ref	–	Reference
rk	–	Rank
SAO	–	Special Army Order
SCM	–	Summary Court Martial
SCN	–	Show cause notice
SFF	–	Special Frontier Force
SGCM	–	Summary General Court Martial
SLP	–	Special Leave Petition
S of E	–	Summary of Evidence
SOP	–	Standard Operating Procedure
Sec	–	Section
Secy	–	Secretary
Stn	–	Station
Tps	–	Troops
Veh	–	Vehicle
W/o	–	Without

PART I

DISCIPLINE, VIGILANCE, COMPLAINTS, PETITIONS AND APPEALS, MAINTENANCE, DEFENCE OF COURT CASES, HUMAN RIGHTS AND ARBITRATION

GOLDEN RULES OF NATURAL JUSTICE

1.	AN ACCUSED IS PRESUMED TO BE INNOCENT TILL PROVED OTHERWISE.
2.	ONUS OF PROVING THE CASE AGAINST THE ACCUSED IS ON PROSECUTION.
3.	NO PERSON CAN BE PUNISHED TWICE FOR THE SAME OFFENCE.
4.	NO ONE TO BE A JUDGE IN HIS OWN CASE.
5.	NO PERSON SHOULD BE PUNISHED UNHEARD.
6.	A DECISION SHOULD INDICATE APPLICATION OF MIND.

PROCEDURE FOR SUBMISSION OF REPORTS REGARDING INCIDENTS AND OFFENCES INVOLVING ARMY PERSONNEL AND FOR THEIR INVESTIGATION

SAO 13/S/80

MAJOR CONTENTS

1. Reporting of incidents and offences
2. Procedure for reporting
3. Investigation of incidents and offences
4. MT accidents
5. Disciplinary proceedings

SALIENT POINTS

1. Reports should be initiated within the stipulated time.
2. Responsibility to initiate the report is not correctly understood.
3. Incidents of minor nature are being reported.

COMMON MISTAKES

1. Delay in reporting.
2. Disciplinary action is started against officers but report is not initiated.
3. SAO is not read properly before initiating report.
4. Not clear when and to whom is the report to be sent.

INVESTIGATION PROCESS

Court of Inquiry is a fact finding body, this is held at a stage prior to commencement of disciplinary action.

COURTS OF INQUIRY

1. Relevant Reference

(a) Army Act section 106

(b) Army Rules 177 to 186

(c) RA (DSR) Paras 516 to 522 and 529

(d) Connotation of the word 'wherever possible' and 'at least'. AHQ Letter No. 46440/AG/DV- 1, dated 11th August, 1983.

(e) Member from the unit concerned — Army HQ. Letter No. 46440/AG/DV-l, dated 28th February, 1991.

2. One man investigation has no legality. May, however, in some cases be held to decide whether probe by C of I is needed.

STAFF OFFICER TO CHECK

1.	Convening order to be approved by the commander before issue.
2.	If a witness is likely to temper with evidence or influence other witnesses, he may be taken into custody.
3.	Confessional statement, if made, to be voluntary and in presence of an independent witness.
4.	In case of assault/affray with Civs, Co-opt a Civ Officer in attendance.
5.	Give information to all concerned to appear as witness.
6.	Findings must be based on evidence.

COMMON MISTAKES

(A)	Being convened in all cases as a routine.
(B)	It involves delay, hence convene only when it is a must.
(C)	Absence of due thought with regard to composition. Members to be carefully chosen having due regard to their rank and seniority.
(D)	Civilians (CDA, MES or DDE officials, etc.) being detailed as members.
(E)	Where required, tech experts not in attendance.
(F)	Delay in procuring attendance of witnesses.
(G)	Being convened by staff offrs.
(H)	Non-compliance of rule 180.
(I)	Practice to make do with a unit C of I when staff C of I is needed.

SALIENT POINTS

1.	Convening offr to ex his mind and ascertain if the character and mil reputation of any offr is likely to be a material issue.
2.	'Wherever Possible' as appearing in RA para 518 cannot be taken as a handle or excuse for not detailing members of the appropriate rank. Relevant factors to decide selection of members are— (a) Rank (b) Suitability and availability to conduct investigation (c) Residual tenure in stn/service (d) No personal interest/connection
3.	Give elaborate and clear terms of ref to avoid ambiguity. This would be help the C of I to carry out the probe thoroughly.
4.	Civilian witnesses can be summoned.
5.	Where possible evidence to be taken on oath.
6.	Rather than a deptl enquiry, hold a C of I.
7.	If required, Court can be reassembled.
8.	If a second or third inquiry is being held, then the covering order must show reason for so doing *e.g.* improper composition of earlier inquiry or need for extended terms of reference.

ARMY RULE 180

(A)	Invoked only when character and military reputation of a person subject to the Act is affected.
(B)	Such person shall be present throughout.
(C)	May cross-examine witnesses.
(D)	May make a statement.
(E)	May produce witnesses in his defence.

COMMON MISTAKES IN FINDING/OPINION

1.	Failure to give clear finding and opinion.
2.	Improper directions like specifying the type and nature of disciplinary/ADM action.

POLICY LETTERS	
Topic	**Army Order/Army HQ letter**
Avoidance of delay in finalisation of court of inquiry proceedings in death cases	AO 16/2000
Cases of unnatural death	46440/AG/DV-1(P) dt 10 July, 1999
Investigation and disposal of general complaints	AO 4/2000
Effect of non-compliance of Army Rule 180 and RA (DSR) Para 518	46440/AG/DV-1(P) dt 15 December, 2000
Finalisation of C of I pdgs, channel to be followed.	53409/AG/DV-1 dt 1 April, 1987
Court of Inquiry – non-compliane of Army Rule 180	46440/AG/DV-1(P) dt 02 July, 2007.

INSTANCES : WHEN C OF I IS OBLIGATORY

(i)	Any loss, damage or destruction of public or regimental property where penal deductions are intended to be imposed.	AA sec. 90 (g)
(ii)	Illegal absence	AA sec. 106
(iii)	Assault and affray, MT accidents resulting in death or serious injury, rape and murder, etc.	RA para 522
(iv)	POW	RA 522
(v)	Loss of Confidential , Secret, Top Secret docu or key	RA 525
(vi)	Unnatural death and suicide, attempted or suspected	RA 529
(vii)	Theft, loss or recovery of arms-ammunition	RA 602
(viii)	Loss or destruction of Regtl docu of JCO, WO and OR	RA 623
(ix)	Loss of stores	RA 903

(x) Suspected loss or damage to a Company or Corporation when a claim against Government may be anticipated.	SAO 14/S/76
(xi) Loss or injury to animals	RA 957(b)
(xii) Fire/Explosives	RA 903, 1195 & 435 and AO 190/79 AI 61/55, 183/58
(xiii) Collective insubordination	SAO 13/S/80
(xiv) Loss of I Card	SAO 2/S/89

HEARING OF CHARGE

Relevant Ref.	
(a) Army Rule	22
(b) AO	24/1994

1. Obligatory, First Step
2. Charge at this stage is a meie accusation
3. Hear min two witnesses
4. Applicable even for summary trials; AHQ Letter No. B/28119/AG/DV-1(P) dt. 5th April, 1999
5. Plea of insanity AO 37/83

POINTS TO REMEMBER

1. Only dispense, if Rule 180 was complied with at C of I stage.
2. Adhere to the procedure contained in AO 24/1994.
3. To be carried out by the CO of the accused.
4. Presence of accused is mandatory.

RIGHTS OF AN ACCUSED

(A) To be present.

(B) To cross-examine witnesses.

(C) To make a statement voluntarily.

(D) To produce witnesses, documents or exhibits in his defence.

PROSECUTION BY CIVIL POLICE

RA (DSR) PARAS	*GIST*
348	Offrs charged with a criminal offence(s) arrested/released on bail and subsequently discharged/acquitted / convicted
357	Assistance to civil auths in criminal cases
416 to 424	Charges by civil power

ARREST

IMPORTANT POINTS

1. Non-intimation about exact date of arrest and release from arrest.
2. Not seeking prior sanction from competent auth for detention beyond 2/3 months.
3. Non-compliance of Army Rule 27 in initiating delay reports.
4. Consideration to withhold pay and allces of arrested pers or those under suspension.

SUMMARY OF EVIDENCE

RELEVANT REF

1. Army Rule 23
2. Memoranda for the guidance of officers concerned with Courts Martial. (Page 436, MML Vol. 2)

SALIENT POINTS

1. Familiarise yourself with all facts of the case.
2. Record only relevant and admissible evidence.
3. Adhere to proper sequence.
4. Put searching and probing questions.
5. Collect evidence on all ingredients of the charge.

DISCIPLINARY ACTION

GENERAL	
MANNER OF DISPOSAL	**AUTHORITY**
1. Summary Trial	AA SEC 80
2. SCM	AA SEC 116 & 120
3. Summary Disposal	AA SEC 83, 84 & 85
4. Courts Martial other than SCM	

	CONVENING	COMPOSITION	POWERS
(a) DCM	Sec 110	114	119
(b) SGCM	Sec 112	115	118
(c) GCM	Sec 109	113	118

PROGRESS OF DISCIPLINARY CASES

COMMON OBSERVATIONS

1. Delay in convening courts martial.
2. Due thought not given to selection of members.
3. Availability of witnesses and necessary exhibits not ensured.
4. Denial of timely access to the accused of—
   (a) Relevant document.
   (b) Defending officer/counsel.
5. Inadequate adm arrangements—
   (a) Secretarial
   (b) Veh
   (c) Accn
   (d) Telephone
6. Verification of service particulars of members and accused for GCM. AHQ Letter No. 35418/AG/DV-1(P) dt 11 Feb and 18 April, 2005.

MOVE OF WITNESSES

COMMON MISTAKES
1. Summons not served through Competent Magistrates.
2. Advance fare not deposited with the Magistrate along with summons.
3. Not adhering to allowed time/move sanction and with-holding witnesses for prolonged duration.
4. All witnesses called at one time. Requirement not anticipated and proper staggering of dates not planned.
5. Demand for witnesses raised at short notice.

HANDLING OF DISCIPLINARY CASES

MAJOR MISTAKES
1. Non or incorrect compliance of AR 22.
2. Lack of jurisdiction for trial of deserters.
3. Detention in mil custody beyond two/three months. Omission to fwd delay report as per AR 27. Not seeking prior sanction of the competent auth for detention beyond two/three months.
4. Lack of care in selection of members of C of I and CM.
5. Non-compliance of AR 115(2).
6. Speaking orders are not issued.
7. Need to adhere to legal provisions is not observed.
8. When in doubt legal advice is not taken from Dy JAG Comd/Corps.
9. Delay in convening courts martial.
10. Availability of witnesses and necessary exhibits not ensured.
11. Accused not afforded due opportunity to prepare his defence.
12. Inadequate adm arrangements.
13. Special considerations shown in case of officers.

ADMINISTRATIVE ACTION

<table>
<tr><td>1. AWARD OF RE-PROOF</td><td colspan="2">RA (DSR) PARA 327</td></tr>
<tr><td>2. AWARD OF CENSURE</td><td colspan="2">AHQ LETTERS No. 32908/AG/DV-1(P), dt. 23rd April, 2007</td></tr>
<tr><td>3. ADM ACTION
(a) Presidential pleasure
(b) Powers of Central Government
(c) Removal or reduction
By COAS and other OFFRS</td><td colspan="2">
AA SEC 18
AA SEC 19, RULE 13A, 14, 15

AA SEC 20</td></tr>
<tr><td>4. RULE 13
RULE 13A
RULE 14
RULE 15</td><td colspan="2">Authorities empowered to authorise discharge.
Termination of service of an Offr by the Central Govt on his failure to qualify at an exam or course.
Termination of service by the Central Government on account of misconduct.
Termination of service by the Central Government on grounds other than misconduct.</td></tr>
</table>

SALIENT POINTS

1. Show cause notice must emanate from the auth proposing to take action.
2. Show cause notice should be explicit like a charge-sheet.
3. Give reasonable opportunity to reply. — All adverse material — Reasonable time
4. Speaking order.
5. For termination of service, limitation period is applicable.

SPEAKING ORDERS

(a) Orders to be issued only after proper application of mind.

(b) Speaking orders prove application of mind.

(c) Otherwise an order may be challenged as—

— arbitrary

— whimsical

— subjective

(d) Elaborate reasons not expected.

(e) Use of vague reasons like 'devoid of merit', 'lacks substance' or 'baseless' is not adequate.

(f) Adopt common sense approach for drafting the order.

(g) Give brief reasons in support of decision, particularly if prayer is being rejected.

(h) No particular format. It would depend upon specific case.

STOPPAGES AND PENAL DEDUCTIONS

Relevant References	
AA Sections	71 (1), 83, 84, 85, 90 and 91.
Army Order	51/1981 (When blamed by a C of I) 25/1983
Policy letter and guidelines	74493/AG/DV-l dt, 12th November, 1993
Pension Regs Part II	Regulation 93 (for recovery of public claim/regimental debt from pension, gratuity or commuted value of pension).

PLURAL MARRIAGE
1. RA (DSR) PARA 333
2. AO 666/1959 and 440/1964
3. ARMY HQ LETTER NO. 79333/AG/DV-1, dt. 6th April, 1998

INSTRUCTION
1. Specific mode of termination must be mentioned in the final order.
2. Action is punitive.

AUTHORITY FOR TERMINATION	
OFFICERS	AA SEC 19 READ WITH ARMY RULE 14
PBOR	AA SEC 20 READ WITH ARMY RULE 17

Action not to be taken under Army Rule 13.

MAINTENANCE

1.	ARMY ACT SECS 90 (i) and 91 (i)
2.	ARMY RULE 193
3.	AO 2 of 2001.
4.	Cr PC, 1973, SEC 125
5.	AHQ Letter No. 79333/AG/DV-1, dt. 22nd March, 1996
6.	Hindu Marriage Act, 1954; section 24
7.	Payments of maintenance allowance to wives and children of Army Personnel under the Army Act AO/2007/DV.

MAINTENANCE

1. Source : By Army Auth or Civil Court
   (A) May extend up to life-time or till—
      (I) Divorce
      (II) Marriage of daughter or till she attains majority.
   (B) May be gross sum or periodical payment.
   (C) May be claimed by both (under the Civil Process as well as army).
   (D) Amount may be varied from time-to-time.

PROCEDURE FOR CLAIMING MAINTENANCE

1. Application by wife or children or on their behalf
2. Application tenable even while matter pending in Civil Court
3. Affidavit with details of—
   (A) Proof of Marriage
   (B) Children
   (C) Property in the name of applicant
   (D) Employment
   (E) Indep source of income
   (F) Willing to stay with husband. If not, brief reasons *e.g.* physical or mental cruelty, torture, etc.

CONDITIONS FOR GRANT OF MAINTENANCE

1.	Legally wedded wife
2.	Husband is neglecting to maintain
3.	Wife unable to maintain herself or children or both

MAINTENANCE MAY BE REFUSED, IF

1.	Sufficient means to maintain
2.	Wife living in adultery
3.	Refusal to live with husband without valid justification

ROLE OF AWWA

1. Counselling
2. Reconciliation and settlement
3. Action to expedite grant of maintenance
   (A) Advice on manner of application
   (B) Scrutinise evidence
   (C) Monitor progress
4. Seek advice from JAG Dept
5. Registration as a Non-Governmental Organisation (NGO)
6. Arrange psychiatric help, if needed

DETAILS TO BE INCLUDED IN THE APPLICATION

1.	Name and address of applicant
2.	Name and address of husband
3.	Personal number of husband and total service
4.	Date of marriage
5.	Rites under which marriage solemnised
6.	Details of children, if any
7.	Period from when husband is not maintaining
8.	Religion of self and husband
9.	Details of employment of applicant
10.	Details of movable/immovable property
11.	Details of source of income of applicant
12.	Signature with date
13.	English or Hindi translation of application, if made in any other language
14.	Detailed reasons for the discord
15.	Affidavit in support for the fact that applicant is the legally wedded wife and does not have any movable/immovable property or any other source of income for her maintenance
16.	Correct address of husband's unit

COMPETENT AUTHORITY

COAS and GOC in C Comd.

AMOUNT OF MAINTENANCE

Not to exceed 33% of pay and allces.

Share of each dependent not to exceed following percentages—

(i)	Wife	22%
(ii)	Each legitimate/illegitimate child dependant on mother who is also being maint	5.5%
(iii)	If wife is not entitled to be maint	25%
(iv)	Child not dependant on mother	25%

MANNER OF AWARD

Specify the sanctioned amount in percentage instead of in exact rupees (Ref AHQ letter No. 79333/AG/DV-1, dt. 22nd March, 1996).

COMMON MISTAKES

1.	Units do not verify facts in adequate detail.
2.	Copies of Court Orders are accepted on face value without verifying contents.
3.	Unattested copies are forwarded.
4.	Recommendations of OC units are not based on supporting documents or evidence.

DISCIPLINE

IMPORTANT POLICY LETTERS

Topic	Army HQ letter No.
1. Trial of deserters	A/21500/MP B(I of R) Coord, dt 24th December, 1999
2. Detention in military custody beyond two/three months	84426/AG/DV-1 (P), dt. 29th September, 1999
3. Non-compliance of mandatory provisions of rules while processing disciplinary cases	35418/AG/DV-1, dt 15th March, 1988, B/28119/ AG/DV-1(P), dt 5th April,

Topic	Army HQ letter No.
	1999 and B/28119/AG/ DV-1(P), dt 27th September, 1999
4. Plural marriage	79333/AG/DV-1(P), dt 6th April, 1998
5. No action to be taken on anonymous/pseudonymous complaints	A/56571/AG/DV-1(P), dt 14th August, 1999
6. Convening orders of GCM/DCM/ SGCM	35418/AG/DV-1(P), dt 13th July, 1999
7. Punishment of dismissal awarded to a JCO/OR can be converted into discharge in deserving cases	48931/AG/DV-1(P), dt 17th July, 1999
8. Termination of service of non-performing re-emp offrs	SAI 1/S/80 read with No 04580/XVII/MS, dt 17th September, 1991
9. Prevention of pilferage of stores from supply depots	50451/AG/DV-1(P), dt 25th May, 1994 and even No., dt 11th June, 1998
10. Policy for dealing with various types of matrimonial cases of officers	79333/AG/DV-1(P), dt 3rd November, 2000
11. Award of censure to officers and JCOs	190105/Censure/R/ A(DV), dt 5th December, 2000
12. No cognizance be taken of directions received directly from NHRC	C/6227/AG/PHRA/ HRC, dt 15th September, 2000
13. Discipline, lady Army officers	5424/AG/DV 1(P), dt 21st August, 2000
14. Types of provisional DV Ban officers	A/56728/AG/DV-1(P), dt 4th July, 2000

Topic	Army HQ letter No.
15. Utilisation of services of JAG's Dept offrs for private purposes is not allowed	B/80518/1075/JAG, dt 26th June, 2000
16. Status of Lance Naik	35418/AG/DV-1(P), dt 21st December, 1999
17. Grant of parole to military convicts undergoing imprisonment in civil jails	49629/AG/DV-1(P), dt 14th December, 1998
18. COS commands and corps empowered to review SCM pdgs	41776/AG/DV-1(P), 23rd November, 1998
19. Action against officers using unauthorised channels for postings	50451/AG/DV-1(P), dt 17th November, 1998
20. Appointment of service personnel as presenting officers in the inquiry proceedings in accordance with CCS (CC&A) Rules, 1965	93792/CCS(CC&A)/ Org 4 (Civ) (a), dt 28th February, 1997
21. Problems of Army personnel with Civil administration	41915/AG/DV-1(P), dt 13th May, 1998
22. Pyrotechnics only to be used for training purposes	50451/AG/DV-1(P), dt 13th May, 1998
23. Detailment of commanding officer on station/courts martial duties	47763/AG/DV-1(P), dt 21st January, 1998
24. Procedure for the removal of undesirable and inefficient JCOs, WOs and OR	13210/159/AG/PS2(c), dt 28th December, 1988
25. Identity cards of JCOs, WOs and OR	AO 12/2000
26. Att of service pers other than offrs to units and fmns nearest to their place of trial in a criminal court	AO 7/2000
27. Instructions regarding norms for official and social functions and adm arrangements	50451/AG/DV-1(P), dt 25th June, 2001

Topic	Army HQ letter No.
28. Furnishing of guest rooms and of appointment houses from regimental funds	A/57035/PS 3(a), dt 3rd March, 1984 A/57035/AG/PS 3(a), dt 3rd March, 1984
29. Commercial activity from govt residential accommodation	AO 376 of 1971, SAO 10/S/1986 72202/AG/DV-1(P), dt 4th December, 2001 and 21st September, 2004
30. Hosting of parties at residence from regimental funds	No. PC/A/57035/EA/AG/PS 3(a), dt 13th April, 2000
31. Acceptance of gifts	RA (DSR) Paras 344, 345 and AO 60 of 1982
32. Rising incidence of litigation by defence personnel	No. 62736/AG-DV-1(P), dt 27th December, 2000
33. SOP for Handling of Suspected Espionage Cases	A/31654/MI-9, dt 31st August, 1999.
34. Grant of Honorarium to Officers detailed as Prosecuting/Defending Officers in GCM	25557/AG/PS-3(a), dt 28th October, 2003.
35. Need for self-contained Speaking and Reasoned Order to be issued by the Authorities Exercising Disciplinary Powers	15420/SPK. Order/MP 4 (Civ) (a), dt 15th December, 2003.
36. Command over Personnel, nomination of OC Troops Information Headquarter	AO 17/2000
37. Persons subject to Army Act serving with or attached to Assam Rifles Units – Command over personnel	AO 18/2000

Topic	Army HQ letter No.
38. Move of Army Personnel in connection with Disciplinary cases	AO 21/2000
39. Indebtedness, Lending, Borrowing of Money and Excessive Drinking	AO 22/2000
40. Medical and Psychiatric examination of an accused remanded for trial by court martial	AO 13/2001
41. Unauthorised Travel in Train by defence personnel	47408/AG/DV-1(P), dt 22nd November, 2004
42. Policy on Administrative Action on Army Personnel involved in espionage activities	38506/AG/DV-1(P), dt 8th February, 2005
43. Discipline/attachment of members of Military Nursing Service (MNS) serving with Air Force/Naval Units or Establishments for the purpose of Disciplinary Proceedings and Administrative Action including the Award of censure	AO 5/2004/DV
44. Misuse of troops, not to be employed for grass cutting or such like menial jobs	50451/AG/DV-1(P), dt 16th March, 2005
45. Discipline of army personnel – behaviour in public and travelling in train	50451/AG/DV-1(P), dt 9th May, 2005
46. Delayed reporting of incidents under SAO 6/5/2000	14887/AG/DV-1(P), dt 12th May, 2005
47. Marriage with foreign nationals	AO 14/2004/MI.
48. Work culture on Sundays/holidays	50451/MISUSE/AG/DV-1(P), dt 22nd September, 2005

Topic	Army HQ letter No.
49. Intimation of the verdict of courts martial to Army HQ	35418/AG/DV-1(P), dt 28th June, 2006
50. Incidents of sexual harassment at work places	50451/SH/AG/DV-1(P), dt 4th July, 2006
51. Discipline of Army personnel: Behaviour in public	50451/AG/DV-1(P), dt 7th July, 2006
52. Delailmen of officers at Mess Functions offrs not to be given demeaning tasks	50451/AG/DV-1(P), dt 7th July, 2006
53. Misuse of I Card by service personnel	A/39201/M1-11, dt 14th July, 2006
54. Discipline of army personnel: behaviour in public while travelling in train	50451/AG/DV-1(P), dt 8th August, 2006
55. Discipline – Arrest/Suspension from Duty	55216/AG/DV-1(P), dt 28 November, 2006
56. Annual leave policy – no denial of leave and no restrictions	13/33922/AG/PS/-2(c), dt 10th January, 2007
57. Reporting of grave incidents	14887/AG/DV-1(P), dt 9th Fabruary, 2007
58. Remedial Measures: Fratricide	A/28019/CAS/GEN/GS/M-4, dt 14th March, 2007
59. Applicability of Army Act section 123	01086/123/AG/DV-1(P), dt 23rd March, 2007
60. Appearance as witness by armed forces personnel before commission of inquiry ordered by State Govts	79627/AG/DV-1(P), dt 16th April, 2007 read with AO 174/77 and 46440/AG/DV-1(P), dt 14th May, 1997
61. Leakage of information to the media, on vigilance and discipline matters	50451/Media/AG/DV-1(P), dt 29th March, 2007

Topic	Army HQ letter No.
62. Indebtedness, lending and borrowing of money. Default in payment of bank loans and credit card dues	AO 22/2000 read with letter No. 50451/AG/DV-1(P), dt 24th April, 2007 and No. 50451/AG/DV-1(P), dt 13th August, 2007
63. Unauthorised leakage of sensitive service information to the media;	A/38007/MI-11, dt 29th May, 2007
64. Wearing of uniform. All individuals not on duty will not wear service uniform	No. B/42703/AG/CW-1, dt 24th July, 2007. Also *see* AHQ No. 13/42901/AG/CW-1, dt 21st Februar, 2007 and 24th December, 2007
65. Provision for Sahayaks to officers, JCOs in the Army	B/32099/AG/PS/-2(c), dt 27th July, 2007
66. C of I in high profile cases which are media glare will be completed in one month time	46440/AG/DV-1(P), dt 29th August, 2007

FINANCIAL IRREGULARITIES AND MISUSE OF RESOURCES

REFERENCE	GIST
RA (DSR) Para 432 read with AHQ letter No. 32908/AG/DV-1(P), dt 16th October, 2000 (Para 3)	Cases of moral turpitude, fraud, theft, dishonesty and culpable negligence involving loss of public or regimental property will be tried by court martial. Such lapses are not to be dealt by award of censure.
AO 570/1959	Financial responsibility to be inculcated throughout the ranks of service and encouragement of cost-consciousness.
SAO 9/S/1976	Loss of regimental funds.
AO 54/1978 AO 110/1978	Competent auth to regularise loss of regimental funds

REFERENCE	GIST
RA (DSR) Para 801 to 832	Cash and Funds incl prevention of fraud and losses of money
RA (DSR) Para 433	Departmental action against government servants who are acquitted by a court of law.
RA (DSR) PARAS 37(j) (i)	Responsibility of a CO for proper application of all public and regimental funds
RA (DSR) Para 317	Obligation to bring dishonesty to notice
RA (DSR) Para 361	Eradication of bribery and corruption
AO 315/1973	Procedure for writing off losses and irregularities and preparation of statement of case.
AO 481/1973	Disposal of audit objections and draft audit paras
AHQ letter No. A/51040/AG/PS-3(d), dt 5th July, 1990	Financial powers for regularisation of losses to regimental funds and stores
AHQ letter No. A/57035/AG/PS-3(a), 8th September, 1994	Administration of Regtl Funds; Powers of various authorities to incur expenditure
Para 243(c) of Stores Accounting Instructions for the Army, 1965	Difference between "neglect" and "gross neglect" as regards losses

MISUSE OF RESOURCES

RA Para 347	The employment of any Government servant, animal, veh or stores for private purposes is prohibited.
RA Para 350	Employment of officers financially embarrassed.
RA Para 361	Eradication of bribery and corruption.

VIGILANCE CASES

Relevant Ref—

(a) RA Paras 357, 361 and 808 (c)

(b) FR Part I Paras 6, 15 and 37

(c) The Central Vigilance Commission Ordinance, 1998.

(d) AHQ letter No. C/00994/6/AG/DV-5, dt 30th September, 1993 and No. 18899/AG/DV-1(P), dt 25th May, 1999.

(e) CVC letter No. 8 (1)(h)/98(l), dt 18th November, 1998.

(f) The Vigilance Manual.

1. Nature of vigilance cases—

   Fraud, misappropriation, bribery, corruption and other malpractices.

2. Features—

   Army personnel fall within the scope of its jurisdiction.

3. Aim—

   (a) To create a culture of honesty.

   (b) Greater transparency in administration.

   (c) Speedy departmental inquiries - use retd offrs, where desirable.

4. Processing of cases in two ways—

   (a) On request from army auth by the CBI.

   (b) On their own.

5. Decision to take up PE (Preliminary Enquiry) is made at the level of SP/DIG/Jt Director/Director CBI either on receiving request or on their own.

6. Brig or above are competent auth to handover a case to CBI.

7. If needed, case be handed over well in time instead of first going through the process of deptl inquiry and then deciding to handover the investigation to CBI. This is a very important aspect which may result in delay.

8. Type of cases which may be handed over to CBI—

   — bribery

   — corruption

   — forgery

   — cheating

   — criminal breach of trust

— falsification of records

— possession of assets disproportionate to known sources of income

— other complicated cases requiring expert police investigation.

9. If verification report indicates a *prima facie* case, it may be registered as a Regular Case (RC).
10. Copy of PE or RC is sent by the CBI to AHQ (AG/DV-5), HQ Comd and concerned Fmn HQ.
11. After registration of an RC, open investigation commences to examine witnesses, etc.
12. Parallel investigation by Army is to be avoided when the matter is with the CBI. Otherwise it may contribute to delay and duplicity.
13. If CBI wishes to carry out surprise check in a unit, prior info will be given to local fmn cdr.
14. Such cases will be reported to AHQ/DV-5 by fastest means.
15. Action when bribe is offered—

    (a) CBI or senior most police/District Officer in station be approached to lay a trap.

    or

    (b) Arrange an independent person to witness the transaction and over hear the conversation between the bribe giver and the bribe taker.
16. Facilities and co-operation be extended to the CBI during investigations—

    — Reports of CBI at conclusion of investigation to be examined by AHQ for deciding the mode of action.

    — C of I to be convened in cases of adm action and recording of S of E to be ordered in cases of discp action, as a result of CBI enquiry.

    — CBI report be given to delinquent with the SCN.

    — Cases to be referred to AHQ where there is disagreement between CBI and Army auth.

    — Concurrence of Central Government necessary for closure of cases investigated by the CBI.

    — Efforts to avoid parallel inquiry in the same case by both the Army and CBI.

IMPORTANT REFERENCES

	ARMY HQ LETTER
Competent Auth to grant or refuse sanction within 30 days for prosecution on a report from CBI and monitoring of CBI Investigations	C/00991/177/AG/DV-4, dt 8th January, 1999

COMPLAINTS, PETITIONS AND APPEALS

1. Ref—
   (i) AA secs 26, 27 and 164
   (ii) RA paras 364 and 365, 370
   (iii) SAO 3/S/1989 and AO 15/1986
2. Features—
   (i) AA Sec 26
   — Remedy of grievances of PBOR.
   — Against any superior or other offr.
   — Remedy by OC in the first instance and finally by the COAS.
   (ii) AA Sec 27
   — Remedy of an aggrieved offr by Central Government.
   (iii) A A sec 164
   — Remedy against order, finding or sentence of court martial by way of Pre-confirmation petition or post-confirmation petition.
   (iv) RA Para 364 complaints.
   — Statutory complaints under AA Secs 26 and 27.
   — Non-Statutory complaint — under authority of AO.
   Number and Extent — Only once to the CO or the Central Government, as the case may be.
   Channel Laid Down — Staff channels.

Action by intermediary auth.

(a) Investigate, where required to verify the facts.
(b) Detailed para-wise comments be prepared.
(c) Give redress, where required.

(d) Grant interview, if needed.

(e) Fwd recommendations.

Time frame for processing complaints.

(a) If no investigation needed	-	135 days
(b) Otherwise	-	80 days
(c) At AHQ	-	45 to 60 days

Final disposal of complaints.

Will be intimated to the complainant directly by disposing auth and the fmn/unit concerned.

A person who has ceased to be subject to Army Act may also file a statutory complaint, within 90 days of his being ceased to be so subject, against any mil wrong done to him when he was so subject.

RA Para 365: Petitions against order, finding or sentence of CM.

(i) May only be addressed by the aggrieved personally, if in service.

(ii) Personally or through duly appointed rep, if not in service.

AUTH TO WHOM PETITION MAY BE ADDRESSED

Before confirmation	Confirming auth.
After confirmation	Central Government, COAS or any auth superior in comd to the confirming auth.
Against SCM	Any auth superior in comd to reviewing auth.

— Aggrieved entitled to file pre and post confirmation petitions, one after the other.

— Auth subordinate to the one to whom petition is addressed may give redressal, if empowered.

Para 370 Appeal against Audit.

— CO who disagrees with the decision of a local audit offr may refer the case direct to the CDA concerned.

— In other cases appeal will be made in writing through bde/ sub-area cdr.

PROCESSING OF COMPLAINTS

COMMON MISTAKES

1. Not proceeded by the Unit/FMN within laid down time-limit
2. Relevant docu are not enclosed by processing Unit/Fmn
3. Copies of classified/official docu are Att
4. Non-monitoring progress of such complaints/petitions

IMPORTANT REFERENCES

GIST	ARMY HQ LETTR No.
Revised format	04480/MS Policy, dt 6th December, 1999
Tenability of complaint by Retd Offrs	62736/AG/DV-1(P), dt 16th December, 1999
No fresh complaint on same matter	62736/AG/DV-1(P), dt 8th March, 1989
Timely processing	B/6003/INF-6(PERS), dt 15th March, 1988
Power of intermediate Cdr to grant relief	62736/AG/DV-1(P), dt 30th June, 2000
Stat complaint not maintainable after cognizance of offence taken	62736/AG/DV-l(P), dt 9th April, 2000
Main points of the complaints be restricted to 2 or 3 pages	37625/POLICY/MS Compls, dt 5th July, 2000
Recommendations/directions must not be signed by a Staff Offr on behalf of a Cdr	C/04697/008/DV-3, dt 14th May, 1998
While processing PCPs/ complaints include details of previous convictions and about accomplices etc.	C/04697/008/DV-3, dt 19th January, 1998

GIST	ARMY HQ LETTR No.
Investigation and disposal of general complaints	AO 1/1997 and 4/2000
Processing of complaints—career matters, JCOs and OR	AO 1/99
Debarrment of officers from initiation/endorsement of CRs being involved in disciplinary cases	A/17151/16/99-MS 4 word, dt 23rd February, 2000
Time Schedule for Processing Statutory Complaints	2736/AG/DV-1(P), dt 30 October, 2004
No action would be taken on third party/proxy complaint	62736/AG/DV-1(P), dt 29th October, 2004
Time-limit for disposal and monitoring of complaints. These to be accompanied by a check list recording the movement of the complaint	04480/MS: Policy, dt 23rd January, 2006
Promotion Policy – an officer will not be given physical promotion till disposal of disciplinary/ administrative action	04502/MS Policy, dt 27th July, 1995

DEFENCE OF COURT CASES

1. Relevant Ref—
   - (a) RA (DSR) Paras 531 to 549
   - (b) SAO 5/5/2001
   - (c) AO 42/1982
   - (d) AI 12 of 1998
   - (e) GOI (Min. of Law) letter No. F No. 26(I)/99-Judl., dt 24th September, 1999.
   - (f) AHQ letter No. 18899/AG/DV-1(P), dt 26th November, 1999.
2. Features:—

(a) No initiation of civil pdgs against the Central Government or a public offr for act done in official capacity w/o notice under CPC section 80. (except Articles 32 and 226 of Constitution).

(b) Sanction for defence or prosecution of a case to be obtained from the competent auth in terms of RA (DSR) para 538.

(c) Engagement of a Government pleader — RA para 542.

(d) Timely filing of counter-affidavit.

(e) Continued attention by unit concerned for progressing the case.

(f) Payment of counsel fee — AI 12/1998.

(g) Timely appeal; if required, to be filed after due approval.

3. Responsibility of various agencies in Court cases.

(a) *OIC Legal Cell.* Ensure effective defence so that a case does not go by default.

(b) *Dy JAG Command.* Adm and professional back up to OIC Legal Cell.

(c) *Local unit detailed or the concerned unit.*

(i) To provide relevant factual inputs to OIC legal cell/ Government counsel.

(ii) To detail a competent offr to study the case and marshal all available material facts.

(iii) Offr so detailed to monitor progress of the case.

(iv) To prepare elaborate parawise comments in consultation with the CO/firm HQ.

(v) Liaise with OIC legal cell, as and when required.

(vi) Funds to meet initial expenses in connection with expenditure incurred in defence/pursuing court cases. Ref AI 12/1998.

(vii) To swear the affidavit.

(d) *Formation HQ.* To provide adm back up to OIC legal cell in the form of man power, tpt, telephone, law books, journals, computer, photocopier, FAX machine and clerical support.

(e) *Directorate at Army HQ*. To monitor the progress of the case and provide factual inputs and actions needed to implement the court orders.

(f) MS Legal, AG/PS, AG/DV or the concerned Dte are responsible for defending and monitoring cases pertaining to them.

(g) *Pension Matters* : Maximum No. of cases pertain to this category (which include family pension, disability pension or war injury pension).

(h) *Accountability for defence of court cases:—*

Responsibility should be fixed for negligent or delayed handling of a court case.

(i) *Cases to be reported to the Government are—*

(i) Contempt cases including those against MOD.

(ii) Where Defence Secy is one of the parties.

(iii) Where interpretation of a rule/regulation/policy is involved.

(j) Prompt action to file appeal/LPA or SLP.

4. Problem areas in dealing with court cases.

(a) Lack of personal involvement by functionaries concerned.

(b) Absence of regular monitoring.

(c) Omission to suitably brief counsels.

(d) Lack of professional approach in representing the case.

(e) Not assigning proper and due importance for the defence of these cases.

(f) Delay in processing with regard to filing of appeal, etc.

5. Consumer forum cases.

POINTS TO REMEMBER

1. Obtain copy of petition or suit at the earliest.
2. Decide whether the case is to be defended.
3. Obtain all relevant info/records.
4. Get para-wise comments prepared.
5. Comply with any interim, stay or other order issued by the court.

6. Liaise with the concerned legal cell regularly.
7. Where required, apply for time extension or for modification of court orders.

IMPORTANT POINTS FOR FMN HQS

Officer detailed to liaise with the legal cells must familiarise himself with facts of the case.

Visualise what all documents/info is needed for contesting the case.

Promptly respond to any communication from legal cells.

Don't send JCOs/OR for swearing counter-affidavits.

Carry adequate cash to meet miscellaneous expenses.

Send original or legible copies of all documents.

IMPORTANT REFERENCES

	ARMY HQ LETTER No.
OsIC Legal Cells not to sign/ affirm/verify counter-affidavits, etc.	B/38277/AG/PS-4(b), dt 10th November, 1998
Processing of claims for compensation for loss of life or injury or damages to property out of traffic accidents involving military vehicles	86107/AG/PS-3(Claims), dt 13th July, 2000 and even, dt 17th May, 2000.
Defence of civil suits/writ petitions in High Courts and the Supreme Court.	
Delegation of financial powers to sanction compensation on the basis of awards of Motor Accident Claims Tribunals	86107/AG/PS-3(Claims), dt 17th May, 2000
MACT Cases	SAO 12/S/65 letter No. 24527/ PS-3(Claims) dt 26th March 1981, 979499, PS-3 (Claims), dt 4th April, 1981, No. 86107/AG/PS-3 (Claims), dt 9th December, 1991 and 8899/AG/DV-1 (P), dt 26th November, 1999.

	ARMY HQ LETTER No.
Delay in implementation of court judgments pertaining to MS matters	04480/MS Policy, dt 22nd February, 2000 and 04480/ MS(ii)/Policy, dt 31st January, 1993
MACT Cases delay in implementation of court judgments, fixation of responsibility and action against erring officials	86107/AG/PS-3(Claims), dt 17th May, 2000
Guidelines containing important legal provisions/instructions, relevant for defence of court cases on MS matters	26052/Misc/MS Legal, dt 17th September, 1993
Handling of court cases – retention of CRDs	04479/MS Policy, dt 7th December, 1999
Dealing with courts and judicial tribunals	AO 15/2003/DV

ARMY ORDERS RELATING TO ANNUAL CONFIDENTIAL REPORTS, ETC.

Medical Fitness	AO 20/75
Acting promotion and retention of acting rank	SAI/1/S/74
Posting/promotion/release retirement orders issued by Military Secretary's Branch	AO 209/76
Instructions for rendering confidential reports on officers	SAO 3/S/89
Annual Medical Examination	AO 18/91
Use of rank after release	AO 320/73

ARBITRATION

Relevant Ref—

(a) Arbitration and Conciliation Act, 1996.

(b) AHQ letter No. 67126/Q/ST-26, dt 24th February, 1997.

Features—

1. (a) Arbitration agreement : may be in the form of an arbitration clause in a contract or in a separate agreement.
   (b) Arbitration agreement to be in writing.
   (c) Process of arbitration may continue even when the issue is pending before a judicial forum as subject of an arbitration agreement.
   (d) Parties free to determine number of arbitrators failing which arbitral tribunal shall consist of a sole arbitrator.
   (e) Arbitrator may be challenged on grounds laid down, *e.g.*, doubts about his independence or impartiality, etc.
2. Conduct of arbitral pdgs—
   — equal treatment of parties.
   — place of arbitration to be decided by parties.
   — pdgs to commence on the date on which a request for a dispute to be referred for arbitration is received by the respondent.
   — language of pdgs to be decided by the parties.
   — statements of claim and defence to be made within the period of time agreed by the parties or determined by arbitrator.
   — claim and reply once filed may be amended or supplemented.
   — hearing and written pdgs to be determined by arbitrator.
   — arbitrator may appoint one or more experts on specific issues to report to him.
   — tribunal to decide the matter in accordance with the terms of contract and usages of trade applicable to the transaction.
   — decision by majority of members where there are more than one arbitrators.
   — arbitrator to encourage settlement by mediation and conciliation, etc.
   — arbitral award to be in writing.
   — recourse against arbitral award—application for setting-aside award to a court.

- — on finality the arbitral award to be enforced as if it was a decree of the court.
- — appeal against orders of arbitral tribunal can be entertained on specified grounds only.
- — the Limitation Act, 1963 shall apply to arbitrations as it applies to pdgs in a court.
- — arbitrator to give reasons for its award.
- — award is equated with the status of a decree. It will no longer be necessary to apply to a court for the decree in terms of the award.

3. Duties and Responsibilities of an Arbitrator:—
   - — to be fair and impartial w/o any bias.
   - — to observe principles of natural justice.
   - — not to misconduct himself or the pdgs.
   - — not to accept any gratification or pecuniary inducement.
   - — to perform duty judiciously.
   - — to give sufficient opportunity to the parties to present their case.
   - — power to proceed *ex parte* if a party does not appear after due notice.

SECTION 18. EQUAL TREATMENT OF PARTIES

1. Rules of Natural Justice
   (A) No one can be a Judge in his own case.
   (B) No one can be punished unheard.
2. Act honestly and impartially.
3. Reasonable and sufficient opportunity.

SECTION 19. RULES OF PROCEDURE

1. Not bound by Civil Procedure Code and Indian Evidence Act.
2. Parties to decide procedure to be followed.
3. (a) Admissibility
   (b) Relevance
   (c) Materiality
   (d) Weight of evidence

SECTION 23. STATEMENT OF CLAIM

1. State facts supporting the claim.
2. Identify points in issue.
3. State relief or remedy sought.
4. Submit all documents.
5. Amend or supplement the claim or defence.

SECTION 24. HEARING AND WRITTEN PROCEEDINGS

1. Decide whether to hold
   (a) oral hearing, or
   (b) based on documents and other material
2. Give sufficient adv notice to the parties about any hearing/ meeting.

GROUNDS FOR REVOCATION OF AUTHORITY OF AN ARBITRATOR

1. Excess or refusal of jurisdiction by the Arbitrator.
2. Misconduct of Arbitrator.
3. Disqualification of Arbitrator.
4. Charges of fraud.
5. Exceptional cases.

SECTION 25. DEFAULT OF A PARTY

1. Without sufficient cause, failure to communicate by the
   (a) claimant of his statement, or
   (b) respondent of his statement of defence.
2. Failure to appear at an oral hearing or to produce docu evidence.

SECTION 26. EXPERTS

To be appointed by the Arbitral Tribunal—

1. One or more in number.
2. To be provided access to—
   (a) docu
   (b) exhibits
   (c) material
   (d) site, etc.
3. Participate in oral hearing.

SECTION 30. SETTLEMENT

Arbitral Tribunal may encourage use of following to bring about a settlement:—

1. Mediation
2. Conciliation
3. Any other procedure

SECTION 31. ARBITRATION AWARD

1. To be in writing and signed by members.
2. Include reasonable rate of interest.
3. Cost of arbitration.
4. May make an interim award at any stage.
5. An application to correct may be made within 30 days for—
   (a) computation error
   (b) clerical or typographical error.

SECTION 34. GROUNDS FOR SETTING ASIDE ARBITRAL AWARD

1. In capacity of a party.
2. Agreement not valid under the law.
3. Want of proper notice or unable to present his case.
4. Matters beyond scope.
5. Improper composition of the tribunal.
6. Subject-matter incapable of settlement.
7. Award in conflict with public policy.

SECTION 37. GROUNDS FOR APPEAL

1. Interim measures under (section 9)
   (a) appointment of guardian;
   (b) preservation, custody or sale of any goods;
   (c) detention, preservation or inspection of any property.
2. Arbitral award itself on the grounds listed in section 34.
3. Jurisdiction (section 16).
4. Interim measure (section 17).

FILING

1. A Ministerial Act.
2. Can be performed by any Arbitrator.

SECTION 31. SIGNING

1. Signature of all Arbitrators.
2. A Judicial Act.

HUMAN RIGHTS

HUMAN RIGHTS CELL (ARMY HQ)

To co-ordinate and apply measures for curbing excesses during anti-insurgency operations. It provides permanent support in order to minimise violations, deny propaganda mileage to militants and counter the growing international criticism of India's Human Rights record.

THE ARMED FORCES (SPECIAL POWERS) ACT, 1958

APPLICABILITY

States of Assam, Manipur, Meghalaya, Nagaland, Tripura, Arunachal Pradesh and Mizoram.

DISTURBED AREA

Central Government or the Governor of the above seven States may, by notification in the Official Gazette declare the whole or part of such States to be a 'Disturbed Area'.

Offrs, JCOs, WO and NCOs of the Armed Forces are empowered to:—

(a) For the maint of public order after giving warning, **fire upon** or otherwise use force, even to the extent of causing death.

(b) **Destroy** any arms dump, prepared or fortified position or shelter or any structure used as a training camp.

(c) **Arrest without warrant** any person who has committed a cognizable offence or against whom a reasonable suspicion exists and may use such force as may be necessary to affect the arrest.

(d) **Enter and search without warrant** any premises to make any such arrest as aforesaid or to recover any person believed to be wrongfully restrained or confined, etc. (Auth section 4 of the Act)

Further under-mentioned powers were to be read in the AFSPA by virtue of the Supreme Court of India's Order dated 7th August, 2001 in Criminal MP No. 500 of 1982 read with *Naga People's Movement of Human Rights* v. *Union of India,* AIR 1998 SC 431.

(a) *Power to Interrogate.*—The Army authorities need not consider themselves restrained from checking information for operational intelligence from an arrestee at the time of his arrest.

(b) *Retention by the Security Forces of the Arms and Ammunition Seized.*—After affecting seizure, the Army authorities should report to the nearest police station about the factum of arrest/seizure furnishing at the same time a list of all confiscated articles and an undertaking to produce the same before the Magistrate concerned. It shall also be necessary for the Army authorities to thereafter obtain orders from the concerned Magistrate for custody of the impounded articles including their interim custody. The custody of the seized property by the Army authorities shall, however, be on behalf of the police concerned, and the same shall be produced by the Army authorities in the court as and when required for the prosecution.

PART II

POWERS OF FORMATION COMMANDERS

LEGAL POWERS OF FMN CDRS
POWERS IN REGARD TO COURTS MARTIAL
SUMMARY POWERS
PENAL DEDUCTIONS
POWERS WITH REGARD TO ADM ACTION
COLLECTIVE FINES
POWER TO GRANT RELIEF
PLURAL MARRIAGE
SUSPENSION OR ATTACHMENT OF OFFICERS
FINANCIAL POWERS
MISCELLANEOUS POWERS

POWER OF FMN CDRS TO APPOINT OC TPS	
Fmn Cdrs empowered to appt OC Tps for all pers of and att to the Fmn HQ	AO 251/1972

POWERS IN REGARD TO COURTS MARTIAL OTHER THAN SCM

ARMY ACT SECTIONS

	Convening	Powers	Confirmation
GCM	109 (A1 warrant)	118	154 (A2 and A3 warrant)
SGCM	112	118	157

Power to claim a case from criminal court for trial under the Army Act. Auth AA section 125 and RA Para 418 as amended *vide* Appx A to AO 109/1978.

SALIENT POINTS

1. Courts Martial are convened without adequate preparation like ensuring availability of all witnesses, documents and administrative arrangements.
2. Frequent queries are made about the type of arrest, release from arrest and leave recommendations for the accused.
3. *Sine die* adjournments made of the proceedings on flimsy grounds without consulting convening or any superior authority.
4. Lack of regular feedback from the unit concerned.

Not to detail an officer with less than three years service as a Judge Advocate for a General Court Martial (Order dated 18th May, 2002 of Delhi High Court in CWP No. 2937 of 1995 in the case of Ex Sep *Ranjit Singh* v. *Union of India*)

POWERS AS CONFIRMING OFFICER

POWER	WITH REGARD TO	AUTH	REFER
1. To confirm the finding and sentence	All ranks	Central Govt. or by any offr empowered in this behalf by warrant of the Central Govt (Usually all indep bde cdrs and above)	AA secs 154, 158 and 182 read with AR 70, 72 and 73

2. To withhold confirmation
3. Reserve confirmation for the superior authority
4. Commute, remit or mitigate any sentence
5. Vary a sentence in excess of law
6. Formally express a sentence which is informally expressed
7. Suspend a sentence of imprisonment for life and direct that the offender shall not be committed to prison or military custody

Note 1. *Commutation.*—is changing the description of punishment by awarding a punishment lower in the scale of punishments.

2. *Remission.*—may be remission of the whole or part of the sentence.

3. *Mitigation.*—is awarding a less amount of the same species of punishment.

EXECUTION OF SENTENCES

POWER	WITH REGARD TO	AUTH	REFER
1. May direct the execution of sentence of RI to be undergöne in civil prison or military custody	All Ranks	Confirming Offr or in the case of SCM the offr holding the court.	AA secs 169 169 read with AR 203
2. May direct execution of imprisonment in civil prison or other fit place in special cases where sentence of RI in military custody cannot be conveniently carried out.	JCOs, WOs and OR	Indep Bde Cdr or above	AA sec 171

ALTERATION OF FINDING AND SENTENCES OF COURTS MARTIAL

POWER	WITH REGARD TO	AUTH	REFER
Alter the Court's finding and sentence which has been confirmed or which does not require confirmation	All ranks	Inep bde cdrs or above	AA secs 163 and 169.

Note 1. A finding may be altered when it is found to be invalid or cannot be supported by evidence. AA section 163(1) refs

2. A sentence may be substituted when it is found for any reason to be invalid. AA section 163(2) refs

POWERS TO SET-ASIDE SCM

POWER	WITH REGARD TO	AUTH	REFER
May set-aside the SCM proceedings or reduce the sentence to any other sentence which the Court might have passed.	NCOs and OR	Bde Cdr and above or any officer empowered by the COAS.	AA sec 162 read with AR 200

Note.—COS Comds and Corps have been empowered *vide* AHQ letter 41776/AG/DV-1(P), dt 23rd November, 1998.

POWERS TO ANNUL COURT MARTIAL PROCEEDINGS

POWER	WITH REGARD TO	AUTH	REFER
May annul the Court martial proceedings on the grounds that they are illegal or unjust	All Ranks	Bde Cdrs and above	AA sec. 165 read with AR 202

POWERS TO ORDER REVISION

POWER	WITH REGARD TO	AUTH	REFER
As confirming officer may order the revision of court's finding or sentence, or both	All ranks	Confirming Offr	AA sec. 160 read with AR 68

Note 1. The finding or sentence may be revised once only. AA section 160 refs.

2. The court may be directed to take fresh evidence. AR 68(2) refs.

POWERS OF PARDON AND REMISSION

POWER	WITH REGARD TO	AUTH	REFER
1. Either with or without conditions pardon the person or remit the whole or part of the punishment, or commute the punishment to a less punishment, or 2. Mitigate the punishment, or 3. With or without conditions release the person on parole	All ranks	Indep bde cdrs or above	AA sec. 179 read with AR 204

SUSPENSION OF SENTENCE

POWER	WITH REGARD TO	AUTH	REFER
1. May suspend the sentence, whether or not the offender already committed to prison or military custody.	All ranks	Offr empowered to convene a GCM or'	AA sec. 182 and 190
2. May, while a sentence is suspended, order— (a) That the offender be committed to undergo the unexpired portion of the sentence, or (b) That the sentence be remitted.	-do-	-do-	AA sec. 186

SUMMARY POWERS

POWER	AUTH	AGAINST WHOM	REF	REMARKS
1. (a) Forfeiture to seniority of rank or of service for promotion up to 12 months	Area or equivalent Cdr and above	Offrs below Lt Col, a JCO or a WO	AA sec. 84 read with AR 26	Right of an accused to elect trial by court martial prior to award under ser 1 (a).
(b) Severe reprimand or reprimand (c) Stoppage of pay and allces				Form 1 and 2 in Part 1 of Appx. IV to AR. (Page 447 of MML Vol II). Also RA Para 444
2. (a) Severe reprimand or reprimand		Bde or equivalent Cdr	Offrs below the rk of Fd Offr, a JCO or WO	AA sec. 83 read with AR 26
(b) Stoppage of pay and allces				

PENAL DEDUCTIONS

POWER	WITH REGARD TO	AUTH	REFER
1. May order withholding of whole or part of pay and allces of person in custody or under suspension on a charge for an offence	JCOs, WOs and OR	Offr empowered to convene a court martial	AA sec. 93 and AR 194
2. Maint of wife, or legitimate or illegitimate child	Offrs and PBOR	COAS and GOC in C	AA sec. 90(i) and 91(i) read with AO 23/1994

POWERS WITH REGARD TO ADM ACTION

POWER	AUTH	WITH REGARD TO	PROVISION	REMARKS
Dismissal or removal from service	Bde Cdrs and above	WOs, NCOs and OR	AA sec. 20 (3) read with AR 17	SCN is obligatory except for special reasons.
Reduction to a lower grade or rank or ranks	-do-	WOs and NCOs	AA sec. 20(4)	-do-
Compulsory discharge	GOC in C	JCOs	AA sec. 22	SCN is obligatory except for special reasons.
-do-	-do-	WOs Class I	AR 13 Table II (iii)	-do-
-do-	Div, Area Bdr or Indep Sub-Area Cdr	Other WOs	AR 13 Table II (iii)	-do-

AWARD OF CENSURE

POWER	WITH REGARD TO	AUTH	REFER
Award of Severe Displeasure and Displeasure	Offrs (incl MNS and re-employed) and JCOs	Divs, Area Cdr and above	AHQ letter No. 32908/AG/DV-1(P), dt 6th October, 2000

IMPORTANT POINTS

1. Show cause notice to be issued only by the competent auth or the staff officer on his behalf and not by the unit or intermediate formation commanders.
2. Procedure when the delinquent is not present to receive the show cause notice or refuses to accept the same is duly explained in the policy letter.

AUTHORITIES WHO CAN AWARD	TYPE OF CENSURE	PERSON TO WHOM AWARDED	RECORDING AND VALIDITY
Central Govt	Severe Displeasure/ Displeasure	Offr/JCO	Permanently recorded in the Dossier
COAS	(i) Severe Displeasure	-do-	-do-
	(ii) Displeasure	-do-	-do-
GOC in C Comd	(i) Severe Displeasure	-do-	-do-
GOC Corps	(ii) Severe Displeasure (Non-Recordable)	-do-	
	(iii) Displeasure	-do-	
GOC Div/Area Comdt Cat A	(i) Severe Displeasure	Offrs	Not recorded
Est, GOC HQ CIF, IG SFF,	(ii) -do-	JCO	Recorded for three years.
IG AR (all not below Maj Gen)	(iii) Displeasure	Offr/ JCO	Not recorded

COLLECTIVE FINES

POWER	WITH REGARD TO	AUTH	REFER
May impose collective fine (after due court of inquiry) for loss of weapon or part of a weapon.	JCOs, WOs, NCOs and OR	Indep Bde or higher Cdr	AA sec. 89 read with AR 185 and 186

POWERS TO GRANT RELIEF

STATUTORY COMPLAINTS

POWER	AUTH	WITH REGARD TO	REFER
May grant redressal of the wrong	All Cdrs	All ranks	AA secs. 26 and 27. RA Para 364

NON-STATUTORY COMPLAINTS

POWER	AUTH	WITH REGARD TO	REFER
May grant redressal of grievance	All Cdrs	All ranks	RA Para 364 (O) and AHQ letter No. 62736/AG/DV-1(P), dt 19th November, 1996

COURTS MARTIAL

POWER	AUTH	WITH REGARD TO	REFER	STAGE
Grant redressal against findings and sentence	COAS or any offr superior in comd to the Confirming Officer	All ranks	AA sec. 164(2)	On receipt of post confirmation petition

REVIEW OF SUMMARY PUNISHMENT

POWER	AUTH	WITH REGARD TO	REFER	GROUNDS
May cancel, vary or remit the punishment or pass any other appropriate direction	COAS or other officer specified by him	Offrs, JCOs and WOs	AA sec. 88 read with RA Para 442	Where the punishment is illegal, unjust or excessive

Illegal.—Contrary to law. It is applicable to everything which is an offence or which is prohibited by law.

Unjust.—Not just, contrary to justice, characterised by injustice.

Excessive.—More than reasonable or necessary, tending to or marked by excess.

RESTORATION OF PENSION/GRATUITY

	AUTH	REF
Power to sanction pension or gratuity or both on submission of an appeal by a PBOR who was earlier dismissed from service.	GOC in C Comd in whose jurisdiction the individual's record office falls.	GOI (MOD) letter No. 12 (6)/95/D (Pen/Sers), dt 9th June, 1999

PLURAL MARRIAGE

Termination of service	JCOs, WOs, NCOs and OR	GOC-in-C Comd	RA Para 333
Grant of *ex-post-facto* sanction to regularise non-obtaining of prior, sanction for contracting second marriage	-do-	-do-	-do-

COMMON MISTAKES

1. Units are not verifying details to adequate extent.
2. Recommendations of oc unit are not based on supporting docu/evidence.
3. Copies of Court orders are accepted on the face value without proper verification. Unattested photocopies are fwd to higher hq for necessary action.

SUSPENSION FROM DUTY OR ATTACHMENT

POWER	AUTH	WITH REGARD TO	REFER
Suspension from duty (independent of arrest)	Offrs	OC or any other superior auth	RA Para 349
Att on disciplinary grounds	Offrs	GOC in C	AI 30/1986

FINANCIAL POWERS TO SANCTION COMPENSATION ON THE BASIS OF AWARD OF MOTOR ACCIDENTS CLAIMS TRIBUNAL

1. GOC in C Comd	Rs. 50,000	in each individual case
2. Corps Commander	Rs. 37,500	-do-
3. Div/Area/Indep Bde/ Sub-Area Commander	Rs. 25,000	-do-
4. Bde/Sub-Area Cdr/ Stn Cdr, Station Cdr, Adm Comdt class I or II	Rs. 12,500	-do-

(Auth: GOI (MOD) letter No. 26(I)/92/D(Pay/Services), dt 30th May, 1994)

FINANCIAL POWERS OF LOCAL COMMANDERS TO GRANT COMPENSATION IN RESPECT OF LOSS OF LIFE OR INJURY OR DAMAGE TO FORCES PROPERTY COMMITTED BY MEMBERS OF THE MILITARY

	Each Individual Case	Max for any one accident
1. GOC in C Command	Rs. 5000	Rs. 50,000
2. Corps Commander	Rs. 3750	Rs. 37,500
3. Div/Area and Indep Bde/ Sub-Area Commander	Rs. 2500	Rs. 25,000
4. Bde Sub-Area/Station Commander and Adm Comdt Cl I or II	Rs. 1250	Rs. 12,500

Auth: GOI (MOD) letter No. 97949/PS3(Claims)/1059/D/Pay/ Services, dt 18th March, 1981

MISCELLANEOUS POWERS

POWER	WITH REGARD TO	REF
1. Appointment of CO for civilians subject to the Army Act	Civilians	AA sec. 7 read with AR 189
2. On active service, to direct retention of an OR sentenced by court martial to dismissal or imprisonment whether combined with dismissal or not	NCOs and below	AA sec. 78 read with AR 191

AIDE-MEMOIRE FOR COMMANDERS

A. Know your powers.

B. Carefully monitor progress of cases.

C. Release accused from arrest unless needed otherwise. Report exact date of arrest and release therefrom.

D. Consult JAG Rep for any advice.

E. Give speaking orders.

F. Introduce accountability.

G. Provide adm back up to legal cells.

H. Interact and maintain harmonious relations with Civil Judiciary.

I. Examine whether pay and allcs of person under arrest/ suspension should be withheld.

PART III

THE ARMY ACT, 1950

THE ARMY ACT, 1950

INTRODUCTION

The Indian Army Act, 1911 was applicable to the regular army in India but its provisions were becoming out-of-date and insufficient for modern requirements. After India attained independence, the need for revision of the Act became imperative. It was, therefore, decided to revise the said Act. To achieve this objective the Army Bill was introduced in the Parliament.

STATEMENT OF OBJECTS AND REASONS

1. The need for a general revision of the three Acts, namely, the Indian Army Act, 1911, the Indian Navy Discipline Act, 1934 and the Indian Air Force Act, 1932, has been felt for some time past. Some of the provisions of the existing Acts were already becoming out-of-date and insufficient for modern requirements, but after the 15th August, 1947, the need for revision became imperative for obvious reasons. It was, therefore, decided to revise all the three Acts with a view to making them self-sufficient and complete codes in themselves. The object was to make them as closely similar in form and arrangement of matter as the special requirements of each service might demand.

2. Although the revision of the Army and the Air Force Acts has been completed, this has not been possible in the case of the Naval Act. The present Naval Discipline Act is modelled on the corresponding British Act which, mainly due to the peculiar traditions of the British Navy, is materially different in many respects from the British Army and Air Force Acts. The revision of the Naval Discipline Act has, therefore, proved a more difficult problem. In the United Kingdom, a special committee has been appointed to examine the question of revision of the British Naval Act. It was felt that it would be an advantage to await the report of that Committee and benefit by its recommendations. The revision of the Naval Discipline Act has, therefore, been suspended for the present. It is expected that the Committee's report will be available within the next few months, after which the revision of the Naval Discipline Act will be taken up. It is, however, not considered necessary to delay the revision of the Army and Air Force Acts any longer and they are, therefore, being introduced during this session of the Legislature.

3. The main objects of the revision of the Army Act are—

(a) to make it self-sufficient by incorporating the relevant provisions from certain other related enactments;

(b) to adapt the existing provisions to suit the new constitutional set-up and present day requirements; and

(c) on the one hand, to bridge the gap between the army and civil laws as far as possible in the matter of punishments for offences and, on the other, to eliminate the disparity between the corresponding provisions of the law governing the Army and the Air Force.

4. The following are some of the more important objects sought to be achieved:—

(1) The Chapter on punishments required to be rationalised. The Indian Army Act, 1911, is on the one hand unduly severe in certain punishments and on the other, inadequate in its enumeration of offences. It also differs considerably from the Indian Air Force Act, 1932 in regard to the scale of punishments for a number of offences. The maximum punishment as now prescribed in the draft Bill, varies with each offence or group of offences as in the Indian Penal Code and other penal laws of the country is in keeping with the gravity of the offence or offences. An attempt has also been made in the Bill to grade punishments according to the gravity of the offences in different conditions, punishments being naturally more severe, for instance, in the case of offences committed wilfully or while on active service.

(2) Provision has been made in the bill for the Indian States forces becoming subject to the Army Act; exclusion of aliens from service except with the consent of the Central Government; grant of commissions to officers; tenure of service at the pleasure of the Governor-General; and safeguards against improper arrest and detention of accused persons before trial. Provisions have been made for minimising chances of injustice of court-martial and, at the same time, for enhancing the status and thereby the responsibility of these courts.

(3) While absolute uniformity is neither possible nor desirable, glaring inequalities have been removed where possible, from the Army and the Air Force Acts. The Bills have been made

identical in form, arrangement and matter with necessary variations in terminology and with such special provisions as were found essential.

(4) The provisions of subsidiary enactments like the Indian Army (Suspension of Sentences) Act, 1920 and Ordinances Nos. XXXVI of 1943 and XXXVII of 1945 relating to penal deductions of pay and allowances of prisoners of war have been incorporated in the Army Bill.

(5) Sections relating to the estates of deceased persons, deserters and lunatics in the Army and Air Force Acts have been omitted. These will form the subject of a separate Bill, common to both the Services.

ACT 46 OF 1950

The Army Bill having been passed by both the Houses of Parliament received the assent of the President on 20th May, 1950. It came into force on 22-7-1950 as THE ARMY ACT, 1950 (46 of 1950).

LIST OF AMENDING ACTS AND ADAPTATION ORDER

1. The Commanders-in-chief (Change of Designation) Act, 1955 (19 of 1955).
2. The Adaptation of Laws (No. 3) Order, 1956.
3. The Repealing and Amending Act, 1957 (36 of 1957).
4. The Repealing and Amending Act, 1974 (56 of 1974).
5. The Air Force and Army Laws (Amendment) Act, 1975 (13 of 1975).
6. The Delegated Legislation Provisions (Amendment) Act, 1983 (20 of 1983).
7. The Army (Amendment) Act, 1992 (37 of 1992).

THE ARMY ACT, 1950

(46 of 1950)

[*20th May, 1950*]

An Act to consolidate and amend the law relating to the government of the regular Army.

BE it enacted by Parliament as follows:—

CHAPTER I

PRELIMINARY

1. Short title and commencement.—(1) This Act may be called the Army Act, 1950.

(2) It shall come into force on such date[1] as the Central Government may, by notification in the Official Gazette, appoint in this behalf.

2. Persons subject to this Act.—(1) The following persons shall be subject to this Act wherever they may be, namely:—

(a) officers, junior commissioned officers and warrant officers of the regular Army;

(b) persons enrolled under this Act;

(c) persons belonging to the Indian Reserve Forces;

(d) persons belonging to the Indian Supplementary Reserve Forces when called out for service or when carrying out the annual test;

(e) officers of the Territorial Army, when doing duty as such officers, and enrolled persons of the said Army when called out or embodied or attached to any regular forces, subject to such adaptations and modifications as may be made in the application of this Act to such persons under sub-section (1) of section 9 of the Territorial Army Act, 1948 (56 of 1948);

(f) persons holding commissions in the Army in India Reserve of Officers, when ordered on any duty or service for which they are liable as members of such reserve forces;

---

1. Came into force on 22-7-1950, *Vide* S.R.O.120, dated 22nd July, 1950, published in the Gazette of India, Pt. II, Sec. 4, p. 86.

(g) officers appointed to the Indian Regular Reserve of Officers, when ordered on any duty or service for which they are liable as members of such reserve forces;

[1][***]

(i) persons not otherwise subject to military law who, on active service, in camp, on the march or at any frontier post specified by the Central Government by notification in this behalf, are employed by, or are in the service of, or are followers of, or accompany any portion of, the regular Army.

(2) Every person subject to this Act under clauses (a) to [2][(g)] of sub-section (1) shall remain so subject until duly retired, discharged, released, removed, dismissed or cashiered from the service.

COMMENTS

Army personnel appearing for entrance examination to Armed Forces Medical College are not amenable to Army Act. Post admission concession and post qualification promotion does not make amenable to Army Act; *Ravi Bhatt* v. *Director General, Armed Forces Medical Services,* AIR 1997 Mad 78.

3. Definitions.—In this Act, unless the context otherwise requires,—

(i) "active service", as applied to a person subject to this Act, means the time during which such person—

(a) is attached to, or forms part of, a force which is engaged in operations against an enemy, or

(b) is engaged in military operations in, or is on the line of march to, a country or place wholly or partly occupied by an enemy, or

(c) is attached to or forms part of a force which is in military occupation of a foreign country;

(ii) "civil offence" means an offence which is triable by a criminal court;

(iii) "civil prison" means any jail or place used for the detention of any criminal prisoner under the Prisons Act,

1. Clause (h) omitted by the Adaptation of Laws (No. 3) Order, 1956.
2. Subs. by the Adaptation of Laws (No. 3) Order, 1956, for "(b)".

1894 (9 of 1894), or under any other law for the time being in force;

[1][(iv) "Chief of the Army Staff " means the officer commanding the regular army;]

(v) "commanding officer", when used in any provision of this Act, with reference to any separate portion of the regular army or to any department thereof, means the officer whose duty it is under the regulations of the regular Army, or in the absence of any such regulations, by the custom of the service, to discharge with respect to that portion of the regular Army or that department, as the case may be, the functions of a commanding officer in regard to matters of the description referred to in that provision;

(vi) "corps" means any separate body of persons subject to this Act, which is prescribed as a corps for the purposes of all or any of the provisions of this Act;

(vii) "court-martial" means a court-martial held under this Act;

(viii) "criminal court" means a court of ordinary criminal justice in any part of India, [2][***]

(ix) "department" includes any division or branch of a department;

(x) "enemy" includes all armed mutineers, armed rebels, armed rioters, pirates and any person in arms against whom it is the duty of any person subject to military law to act;

(xi) "the Forces" means the regular Army, Navy and Air Force or any part of any one or more of them;

(xii) "junior commissioned officer" means a person commissioned, gazetted or in pay as a junior commissioned officer in the regular Army or the Indian Reserve Forces, and includes a person holding a junior commission in the Indian Supplementary Reserve Forces, or the Territorial Army, [3][***] who is for the time being subject to this Act;

---

1. Subs. by Act 19 of 1955, sec. 2 and Sch., for the original clause.
2. The words "other than the State of Jammu and Kashmir" omitted by Act 13 of 1975, sec. 3.
3. The words "or a junior or equivalent commission in the land forces of a Part B State" omitted by the Adaptation of Laws (No. 3) Order, 1956.

(xiii) "military custody" means the arrest or confinement of a person according to the usages of the service and includes naval or air force custody;

(xiv) "military reward" includes any gratuity or annuity for long service or good conduct, good service pay or pension, and any other military pecuniary reward;

(xv) "non-commissioned officer" means a person holding a non-commissioned rank or an acting non-commissioned rank in the regular Army or the Indian Reserve Forces, and includes a non-commissioned officer or acting non-commissioned officer of the Indian Supplementary Reserve Forces or the Territorial Army, [1][***] who is for the time being subject to this Act;

(xvi) "notification" means a notification published in the Official Gazette;

(xvii) "offence" means any act or omission punishable under this Act and includes a civil offence as hereinbefore defined;

(xviii) "officer" means a person commissioned, gazetted or in pay as an officer in the regular Army, and includes—

(a) an officer of the Indian Reserve Forces;

(b) an officer holding a commission in the Territorial Army granted by the President with designation of rank corresponding to that of an officer of the regular Army who is for the time being subject to this Act;

(c) an officer of the Army in India Reserve of Officers who is for the time being subject to this Act;

(d) an officer of the Indian Regular Reserve of Officers who is for the time being subject to this Act;

[2][***]

(f) in relation to a person subject to this Act when serving under such conditions as may be prescribed, an officer of the Navy or Air Force;

---

1. The words "or the land forces of a Part B State" omitted by the Adaptation of Laws (No. 3) Order, 1956.
2. Sub-clause (e) omitted by the Adaptation of Laws (No. 3) Order, 1956.

but does not include a junior commissioned officer, warrant officer, petty officer or non-commissioned officer;

(xix) "prescribed" means prescribed by rules made under this Act;

(xx) "provost-marshal" means a person appointed as such under section 107 and includes any of his deputies or assistants or any other person legally exercising authority under him or on his behalf;

(xxi) "regular Army" means officers, junior commissioned officers, warrant officers, non-commissioned officers and other enrolled persons who, by their commission, warrant, terms of enrolment or otherwise are liable to render continuously for a term military service to the Union in any part of the world, including persons belonging to the Reserve Forces and the Territorial Army when called out on permanent service;

(xxii) "regulation" includes a regulation made under this Act;

(xxiii) "superior officer", when used in relation to a person subject to this Act, includes a junior commissioned officer, warrant officer and a non-commissioned officer, and, as regards persons placed under his orders, an officer, warrant officer, petty officer and non-commissioned officer of the Navy or Air Force;

(xxiv) "warrant officer" means a person appointed, gazetted or in pay as a warrant officer of the regular Army or of the Indian Reserve Forces, and includes a warrant officer of the Indian Supplementary Reserve Forces or of the Territorial Army [1][***] who is for the time being subject to this Act;

(xxv) [2][all words (except the word "India")] and expressions used but not defined in this Act and defined in the Indian Penal Code (45 of 1860) shall be deemed to have the meanings assigned to them in that Code.

---

1. The words "or of the land forces of a Part B State" omitted by the Adaptation of Laws (No. 3) Order, 1956.
2. Subs. by Act 13 of 1975, sec. 3, for "all words".

CHAPTER II

SPECIAL PROVISIONS FOR THE APPLICATION OF ACT IN CERTAIN CASES

4. Application of Act to certain forces under Central Government.—(1) The Central Government may, by notification, apply, with or without modifications, all or any of the provisions of this Act to any force raised and maintained in India under the authority of that Government [1][***] and suspend the operation of any other enactment for the time being applicable to the said force.

(2) The provisions of this Act so applied shall have effect in respect of persons belonging to the said force as they have effect in respect of persons subject to this Act holding in the regular Army the same or equivalent rank as the aforesaid persons hold for the time being in the said force.

(3) The provisions of this Act so applied shall also have effect in respect of persons who are employed by or are in the service of or are followers of or accompany any portion of the said force as they have effect in respect of persons subject to this Act under [2][clause (i) of sub-section (1) of section 2].

(4) While any of the provisions of this Act apply to the said force, the Central Government may, by notification, direct by what authority any jurisdiction, powers or duties incident to the operation of these provisions shall be exercised or performed in respect of the said force.

COMMENTS

In exercise of the powers conferred by sub-sections (1) and (4) of section 4 of the Act, the Central Government hereby—

(1) applies to the Rashtriya Rifles, being a Force raised and maintained in India under the authority of the Central Government, all the provisions of the said Act; and

(2) directs that the authority mentioned in the first column of the table below, shall exercise or perform in respect of members of the said Force under his command the

---

1. The words "including any force maintained by a Part B State" omitted by the Adaptation of Laws (No. 3) Order, 1956.

2. Subs. by Act 56 of 1974, sec. 3 and Sch. II, for "clause (i) of section 2".

jurisdiction, powers and duties incident to the operation of the provisions of the said Act specified in the second column thereof:

TABLE

Authority	**Juridication, powers and duties**
Sector Commander of Rashtriya Rifles	Those of an officer commanding a Brigade.

5. Application of Act to forces of Part B States.—[*Rep. by the Adaptation of Laws (No. 3) Order, 1956.*]

6. Special provision as to rank in certain cases.—(1) The Central Government may, by notification, direct that any person or class of persons subject to this Act under [1][clause (i) of sub-section (1) of section 2] shall be so subject as officers, junior commissioned officers, warrant officers or non-commissioned officers and may authorise any officer to give a like direction and to cancel such direction.

(2) All persons subject to this Act other than officers, junior commissioned officers, warrant officers and non-commissioned officers shall, if they are not persons in respect of whom a notification or direction under sub-section (1) is in force, be deemed to be of rank inferior to that of a non-commissioned officer.

7. Commanding officer of persons subject to military law under clause (i) of section 2.—(1) Every person subject to this Act under [1][clause (i) of sub-section (1) of section 2] shall, for the purposes of this Act, be deemed to be under the commanding officer of the corps, department or detachment, if any, to which he is attached, and, if he is not so attached, under the command of any officer who may for the time being be named as his commanding officer by the officer commanding the force with which such person for the time being is serving, or any other prescribed officer, or, if no such officer is named or prescribed, under the command of the said officer commanding the force.

(2) An officer commanding a force shall not place a person subject to this Act under [1][clause (i) of sub-section (1) of section 2] under the command of an officer of rank inferior to that of such

1. Subs. by Act 56 of 1974, sec. 3 and Sch. II, for "clause (i) of section 2".

person, if there is present at the place where such person is any officer of a higher rank under whose command he can be placed.

8. Officers exercising powers in certain cases.—(1) Whenever persons subject to this Act are serving under an officer commanding any military organisation, not in this section specifically named and being in the opinion of the Central Government not less than a brigade, that Government may prescribe the officer by whom the powers, which under this Act may be exercised by officers commanding armies, army corps, divisions and brigades, shall, as regards such persons, be exercised.

(2) The Central Government may confer such powers, either absolutely or subject to such restrictions, reservations, exceptions and conditions, as it may think fit.

9. Power to declare persons to be on active service.—Notwithstanding anything contained in clause (i) of section 3, the Central Government may, by notification, declare that any person or class of persons subject to this Act shall, with reference to any area in which they may be serving or with reference to any provision of this Act or of any other law for the time being in force, be deemed to be on active service within the meaning of this Act.

COMMENTS

In exercise of the powers conferred by section 9 of the Act, the Central Government hereby declares that all persons subject to the Act, who are not on active service under clause (i) of section 3, shall, while serving with the Army Farms and Units deployed on Operation RAKSHAK in the States of Punjab, Jammu and Kashmir, Rajasthan, Gujarat and the Union Territory of Chandigarh be deemed to be on active service within the meaning of the Act and of any other law for the time being in force.

CHAPTER III

COMMISSION, APPOINTMENT AND ENROLMENT

10. Commission and appointment.—The President may grant, to such person as he thinks fit, a commission as an officer, or as a junior commissioned officer or appoint any person as a warrant officer of the regular Army.

11. Ineligibility of aliens for enrolment.—No person who is not a citizen of India shall, except with the consent of the Central Government signified in writing, be enrolled in the regular Army:

Provided that nothing contained in this section shall bar the enrolment of the subjects of Nepal in the regular Army.

12. Ineligibility of females for enrolment or employment.— No female shall be eligible for enrolment or employment in the regular Army, except in such corps, department, branch or other body forming part of, or attached to any portion of, the regular Army as the Central Government may, by notification in the Official Gazette, specify in this behalf:

Provided that nothing contained in this section shall affect the provisions of any law for the time being in force providing for the raising and maintenance of any service auxiliary to the regular Army or any branch thereof in which females are eligible for enrolment or employment.

13. Procedure before enrolling officer.—Upon the appearance before the prescribed enrolling officer of any person desirous of being enrolled, the enrolling officer shall read and explain to him, or cause to be read and explained to him in his presence, the conditions of the service for which he is to be enrolled; and shall put to him the questions set forth in the prescribed form of enrolment, and shall, after having cautioned him that if he makes a false answer to any such question he will be liable to punishment under this Act, record or cause to be recorded his answer to each such question.

14. Mode of enrolment.—If, after complying with the provisions of section 13, the enrolling officer is satisfied that the person desirous of being enrolled fully understands the questions put to him and consents to the conditions of service, and if such officer perceives no impediment, he shall sign and shall also cause such person to sign the enrolment paper, and such person shall thereupon be deemed to be enrolled.

15. Validity of enrolment.—Every person who has for the space of three months been in receipt of pay as a person enrolled under this Act and been borne on the rolls of any corps or department shall be deemed to have been duly enrolled, and shall not be entitled to claim his discharge on the ground of any irregularity or illegality in his enrolment or on any other ground whatsoever; and if any person, in receipt of such pay and borne on the rolls as aforesaid, claims his discharge before the expiry of three months from his enrolment, no such irregularity or illegality or other ground shall, until he is discharged in pursuance of his claim, affect his position as an enrolled person under this Act or invalidate any proceeding, act or thing taken or done prior to his discharge.

16. Persons to be attested.—The following persons shall be attested, namely:—

(a) all persons enrolled as combatants;

(b) all persons selected to hold a non-commissioned or acting non-commissioned rank; and

(c) all other persons subject to this Act as may be prescribed by the Central Government.

17. Mode of attestation.—(1) When a person who is to be attested is reported fit for duty, or has completed the prescribed period of probation, an oath or affirmation shall be administered to him in the prescribed form by his commanding officer in front of this corps or such portion thereof or such members of his department as may be present, or by any other prescribed person.

(2) The form of oath or affirmation prescribed under this section shall contain a promise that the person to be attested will bear true allegiance to the Constitution of India as by law established, and that he will serve in the regular Army and go wherever he is ordered by land, sea or air, and that he will obey all commands of any officer set over him, even to the peril of his life.

(3) The fact of an enrolled person having taken the oath or affirmation directed by this section to be taken shall be entered on his enrolment paper, and authenticated by the signature of the officer administering the oath or affirmation.

CHAPTER IV

CONDITIONS OF SERVICE

18. Tenure of service under the Act.—Every person subject to this Act shall hold office during the pleasure of the President.

19. Termination of service by Central Government.—Subject to the provisions of this Act and the rules and regulations made thereunder the Central Government may dismiss, or remove from the service, any person subject to this Act.

20. Dismissal, removal or reduction by the Chief of the Army Staff and by other officers.—(1) [1][The Chief of the Army Staff] may dismiss or remove from the service any person subject to this Act, other than an officer.

(2) [1][The Chief of the Army Staff] may reduce to a lower grade or rank or the ranks, any warrant officer or any non-commissioned officer.

(3) An officer having power not less than a brigade or equivalent commander or any prescribed officer may dismiss or remove from the service any person serving under his command other than an officer or a junior commissioned officer.

(4) Any such officer as is mentioned in sub-section (3) may reduce to a lower grade or rank or the ranks, any warrant officer or any non-commissioned officer under his command.

(5) A warrant officer reduced to the ranks under this section shall not, however, be required to serve in the ranks as a sepoy.

(6) The commanding officer of an acting non-commissioned officer may order him to revert to his permanent grade as a non-commissioned officer, or if he has no permanent grade above the ranks, to the ranks.

(7) The exercise of any power under this section shall be subject to the said provisions contained in this Act and the rules and regulations made thereunder.

21. Power to modify certain fundamental rights in their application to persons subject of this Act.—Subject to the provisions of any law for the time being in force relating to the regular Army or to any branch thereof, the Central Government may, by notification, make rules restricting to such extent and in such manner as may be necessary the right of any person subject to this Act—

(a) to be a member of, or to be associated in any way with, any trade union or labour union, or any class of trade or labour unions, or any society, institution or association or any class of institution or associations;

(b) to attend or address any meeting or to take part in any demonstration organised by any body of persons for any political or other purposes;

---

1. Subs. by Act 19 of 1955, sec. 2 and Sch., for "The Commander-in-Chief".

(c) to communicate with the press or to publish or cause to be published any book, letter or other document.

22. Retirement, release or discharge.—Any person subject to this Act may be retired, released or discharged from the service by such authority and in such manner as may be prescribed.

23. Certificate on termination of service.—Every junior commissioned officer, warrant officer, or enrolled person who is dismissed, removed, discharged, retired or released from the service shall be furnished by his commanding officer with a certificate, in the language which is the mother tongue of such person and also in the English language setting forth—

(a) the authority terminating his service;

(b) the cause for such termination; and

(c) the full period of his service in the regular Army.

24. Discharge or dismissal when out of India.—(1) Any person enrolled under this Act who is entitled under the conditions of his enrolment to be discharged, or whose discharge is ordered by competent authority, and who, when he is so entitled or ordered to be discharged, is serving out of India, and requests to be sent to India, shall, before being discharged, be sent to India with all convenient speed.

(2) Any person enrolled under this Act who is dismissed from the service and who, when he is so dismissed, is serving out of India, shall be sent to India with all convenient speed.

(3) Where any such person as is mentioned in sub-section (2) is sentenced to dismissal combined with any other punishment, such other punishment, or, in the case of a sentence of transportation or imprisonment, a portion of such sentence may be inflicted before he is sent to India.

(4) For the purposes of this section, the word "discharge" shall include release, and the word "dismissal" shall include removal.

CHAPTER V

SERVICE PRIVILEGES

25. Authorised deductions only to be made from pay.—The pay of every person subject to this Act due to him as such under any regulation for the time being in force shall be paid without any deduction other than the deductions authorised by or under this or any other Act.

26. Remedy of aggrieved persons other than officers.—(1) Any person subject to this Act other than an officer who deems himself wronged by any superior or other officer may, if not attached to a troop or company, complain to the officer under whose command or orders he is serving; and may, if attached to a troop or company, complain to the officer commanding the same.

(2) When the officer complained against is the officer to whom any complaint should, under sub-section (1), be preferred, the aggrieved person may complain to such officer's next superior officer.

(3) Every officer receiving any such complaint shall make as complete an investigation into it as may be possible for giving full redress to the complainant; or, when necessary, refer the complaint to superior authority.

(4) Every such complaint shall be preferred in such manner as may from time to time be specified by the proper authority.

(5) The Central Government may revise any decision by [1][the Chief of the Army Staff] under sub-section (2), but, subject thereto, the decision of [1][the Chief of the Army Staff] shall be final.

27. Remedy of aggrieved officers.—Any officer who deems himself wronged by his commanding officer or any superior officer and who on due application made to his commanding officer does not receive the redress to which he considers himself entitled, may complain to the Central Government in such manner as may from time to time be specified by the proper authority.

28. Immunity from attachment.—Neither the arms, clothes, equipment, accoutrements or necessaries of any person subject to this Act, nor any animal used by him for the discharge of his duty, shall be seized, nor shall the pay and allowances of any such person or any part thereof be attached, by direction of any civil or revenue court or any revenue officer in satisfaction of any decree or order enforceable against him.

29. Immunity from arrest for debt.—(1) No person subject to this Act shall, so long as he belongs to the Forces, be liable to be arrested for debt under any process issued by, or by the authority of, any civil or revenue court or revenue officer.

---

1. Subs. by Act 19 of 1955, sec. 2 and Sch., for "The Commander-in-Chief".

(2) The judge of any such court or the said officer may examine into any complaint made by such person or his superior officer of the arrest of such person contrary to the provisions of this section and may, by warrant under his hand, discharge the person, and award reasonable costs to the complainant, who may recover those costs in like manner as he might have recovered costs awarded to him by a decree against the person obtaining the process.

(3) For the recovery of such costs no court-fee shall be payable by the complainant.

30. Immunity of persons attending courts-martial from arrest.—(1) No presiding officer or member of a court-martial, no judge-advocate, no party to any proceeding before a court-martial, or his legal practitioner or agent, and no witness acting in obedience to a summons to attend a court-martial shall, while proceeding to, attending, or returning from, a court-martial, be liable to arrest under civil or revenue process.

(2) If any such person is arrested under any such process, he may be discharged by order of the court-martial.

31. Privileges of reservists.—Every person belonging to the Indian Reserve Forces shall, when called out for or engaged in or returning from, training or service, be entitled to all the privileges accorded by sections 28 and 29 to a person subject to this Act.

32. Priority in respect of army personnel's litigation.—(1) On the presentation to any court by or on behalf of any person subject to this Act of a certificate from the proper military authority of leave of absence having been granted to or applied for by him for the purpose of prosecuting or defending any suit or other proceeding in such court, the court shall, on the application of such person, arrange, so far as may be possible, for the hearing and final disposal of such suit or other proceeding within the period of the leave so granted or applied for.

(2) The certificate from the proper military authority shall state the first and last day of the leave for intended leave, and set forth a description of the case with respect to which the leave was granted or applied for.

(3) No fee shall be payable to the court in respect of the presentation of any such certificate, or of any application by or on behalf of any such person, for priority for the hearing of his case.

(4) Where the court is unable to arrange for the hearing and final disposal of the suit or other proceeding within the period of such leave or intended leave as aforesaid, it shall record its reasons for its inability to do so, and shall cause a copy thereof to be furnished to such person on his application without any payment whatever by him in respect either of the application for such copy or of the copy itself.

(5) If in any case a question arises as to the proper military authority qualified to grant such certificate as aforesaid, such question shall at once be referred by the court to an officer having power not less than a brigade or equivalent commander whose decision shall be final.

33. Saving of rights and privileges under other laws.—The rights and privileges specified in the preceding sections of this Chapter shall be in addition to, and not in derogation of, any other rights and privileges conferred on persons subject to this Act or on members of the regular Army, Navy and Air Force generally by any other law for the time being in force.

CHAPTER VI

OFFENCES

34. Offences in relation to the enemy and punishable with death.—Any person subject to this Act who commits any of the following offences, that is to say,—

(a) shamefully abandons or delivers up any garrison, fortress, post, place or guard, committed to his charge, or which it is his duty to defend, or uses any means to compel or induce any commanding officer or other person to commit any of the said acts; or

(b) intentionally uses any means to compel or induce any person subject to military, naval or air force law to abstain from acting against the enemy, or to discourage such person from acting against the enemy; or

(c) in the presence of the enemy, shamefully casts away his arms, ammunition, tools or equipment or misbehaves in such manner as to show cowardice; or

(d) treacherously holds correspondence with, or communicates intelligence to, the enemy or any person in arms against the Union; or

(e) directly or indirectly assists the enemy with money, arms, ammunition, stores or supplies; or

(f) treacherously or through cowardice sends a flag of truce to the enemy; or

(g) in time of war or during any military operation, intentionally occasions a false alarm in action, camp, garrison or quarters, or spreads reports calculated to create alarm or despondency; or

(h) in time of action leaves his commanding officer or his post, guard, picquet, patrol or party without being regularly relieved or without leave; or

(i) having been made a prisoner of war, voluntarily serves with or aids the enemy; or

(j) knowingly harbours or protects an enemy not being a prisoner; or

(k) being a sentry in time of war or alarm, sleeps upon his post or is intoxicated; or

(l) knowingly does any act calculated to imperil the success of the military, naval or air forces of India or any forces co-operating therewith or any part of such forces,

shall, on conviction by court-martial be liable to suffer death or such less punishment as is in this Act mentioned.

COMMENTS

Appellant, on the militants opening fire, shamefully abandoned the place committed to his charge and which he was under a duty to defend attracts clauses (a) and (h) of section 34. Trial should be by court-martial and not summary court-martial; *Ex-Havildar Rattan Singh* v. *Union of India*, AIR 1992 SC 415.

35. Offences in relation to the enemy and not punishable with death.—Any person subject to this Act who commits any of the following offences, that is to say,—

(a) is taken prisoner, by want of the precaution, or through disobedience of orders, or wilful neglect of duty, or having been taken prisoner, fails to rejoin his service when able to do so; or

(b) without due authority holds correspondence with or communicates intelligence to the enemy or having come by the knowledge of any such correspondence or communication, wilfully omits to discover it immediately to his commanding or other superior officer; or

(c) without due authority sends a flag of truce to the enemy,

shall, on conviction by court-martial, be liable to suffer imprisonment for a term which may extend to fourteen years or such less punishment as is in this Act mentioned.

36. Offences punishable more severely on active service than at other times.—Any person subject to this Act who commits any of the following offences, that is to say,—

(a) forces a safeguard, or forces or uses criminal force to a sentry; or

(b) breaks into any house or other place in search of plunder; or

(c) being a sentry sleeps upon his post, or is intoxicated; or

(d) without orders from his superior officer leaves his guard, picquet, patrol or post; or

(e) intentionally or through neglect occasions a false alarm in camp, garrison, or quarters; or spreads reports calculated to create unnecessary alarm or despondency; or

(f) makes known the parole, watchword or countersign to any person not entitled to receive it; or knowingly gives a parole, watchword or countersign different from what he received,

shall, on conviction by court-martial,

if he commits any such offence when on active service, be liable to suffer imprisonment for a term which may extend to fourteen years or such less punishment as is in this Act mentioned; and

if he commits any such offence when not on active service, be liable to suffer imprisonment for a term which may extend to seven years or such less punishment as is in this Act mentioned.

37. Mutiny.—Any person subject to this Act who commits any of the following offences, that is to say,—

(a) begins, incites, causes, or conspires with any other person to cause any mutiny in the military, naval or air forces of India or any forces co-operating therewith; or

(b) joins in any such mutiny; or

(c) being present at any such mutiny, does not use his utmost endeavours to suppress the same; or

(d) knowing or having reason to believe in the existence of any such mutiny, or of any intention to mutiny, or of any such conspiracy, does not, without delay, give information thereof to his commanding or other superior officer; or

(e) endeavours to seduce any person in the military, naval or air forces of India from his duty or allegiance to the Union,

shall, on conviction by court-martial, be liable to suffer death or such less punishment as is in this Act mentioned.

38. Desertion and aiding desertion.—(1) Any person subject to this Act who deserts or attempts to desert the service shall, on conviction by court-martial,

if he commits the offence on active service or when under orders for active service, be liable to suffer death or such less punishment as is in this Act mentioned; and

if he commits the offence under any other circumstances, be liable to suffer imprisonment for a term which may extend to seven years or such less punishment as is in this Act mentioned.

(2) Any person subject to this Act who, knowingly harbours any such deserter shall, on conviction by court-martial, be liable to suffer imprisonment for a term which may extend to seven years or such less punishment as is in this Act mentioned.

(3) Any person subject to this Act, who, being cognizant of any desertion or attempt at desertion of a person subject to this Act, does not forthwith give notice to his own or some other superior officer, or take any steps in his power to cause such person to be apprehended, shall, on conviction by court-martial, be liable to suffer imprisonment for a term which may extend to two years or such less punishment as is in this Act mentioned.

39. Absence without leave.—Any person subject to this Act who commits any of the following offences, that is to say,—

(a) absents himself without leave; or

(b) without sufficient cause overstays leave granted to him; or

(c) being on leave of absence and having received information from proper authority that any corps, or portion of a corps, or any department, to which he belongs, has been ordered on active service, fails, without sufficient cause, to rejoin without delay; or

(d) without sufficient cause fails to appear at the time fixed at the parade or place appointed for exercise or duty; or

(e) when on parade, or on the line of march, without sufficient cause or without leave from his superior officer, quits the parade or line or march; or

(f) when in camp or garrison or elsewhere, is found beyond any limits fixed, or in any place prohibited, by any general, local or other order, without a pass or written leave from his superior officer; or

(g) without leave from his superior officer or without due cause, absents himself from any school when duly ordered to attend there,

shall, on conviction by court-martial, be liable to suffer imprisonment for a term which may extend to three years or such less punishment as is in this Act mentioned.

40. Striking or threatening superior officers.—Any person subject to this Act who commits any of the following offences, that is to say,—

(a) uses criminal force to or assaults his superior officer; or

(b) uses threatening language to such officer; or

(c) uses insubordinate language to such officer,

shall, on conviction by court-martial,

if, such officer is at the time in the execution of his office or, if the offence is committed on active service, be liable to suffer imprisonment for a term which may extend to fourteen years or such less punishment as is in this Act mentioned; and

in other cases, be liable to suffer imprisonment for a term which may extend to ten years or such less punishment as is in this Act mentioned:

Provided that in the case of an offence specified in clause (c), the imprisonment shall not exceed five years.

41. Disobedience to superior officer.—(1) Any person subject to this Act who disobeys in such manner as to show a wilful defiance of authority any lawful command given personally by his superior officer in the execution of his office whether the same is given orally, or in writing or by signal or otherwise, shall, on conviction by court-martial, be liable to suffer imprisonment for a term which may extend to fourteen years or such less punishment as is in this Act mentioned.

(2) Any person subject to this Act who disobeys any lawful command given by his superior officer shall, on conviction by court-martial,

if he commits such offence when on active service, be liable to suffer imprisonment for a term which may extend to fourteen years or such less punishment as is in this Act mentioned; and

if he commits such offence when not on actives service, be liable to suffer imprisonment for a term which may extend to five years or such less punishment as is in this Act mentioned.

42. Insubordination and obstruction.—Any person subject to this Act who commits any of the following offences, that is to say,—

(a) being concerned in any quarrel, affray, or disorder, refuses to obey any officer, though of inferior rank, who orders him into arrest, or uses criminal force to or assaults any such officer; or

(b) uses criminal force to, or assaults any person, whether subject to this Act or not, in whose custody he is lawfully placed, and whether he is or is not his superior officer; or

(c) resists an escort whose duty it is to apprehend him or to have him in charge; or

(d) breaks out of barracks, camp or quarters; or

(e) neglects to obey any general, local or other order; or

(f) impedes the provost-marshal or any person lawfully acting on his behalf, or when called upon, refuses to assist in the execution of his duty a provost-marshal or any person lawfully acting on his behalf; or

(g) uses criminal force to or assaults any person bringing provisions or supplies to the forces,

shall, on conviction by court-martial, be liable to suffer imprisonment for a term which may extend, in the case of the offences specified in clauses (d) and (e) to two years, and in the case of the offences specified in the other clauses to ten years, or such less punishment as is in this Act mentioned.

43. Fraudulent enrolment.—Any person subject to this Act who commits any of the following offences, that is to say,—

(a) without having obtained a regular discharge from the corps or department to which he belongs, or otherwise fulfilled the conditions enabling him to enrol or enter, enrols himself in, or enters the same or any other corps or department or any part of the naval or air forces of India or the Territorial Army; or

(b) is concerned in the enrolment in any part of the Forces of any person when he knows or has reason to believe such person to be so circumstanced that by enrolling he commits an offence against this Act,

shall, on conviction by court-martial, be liable to suffer imprisonment for a term which may extend to five years or such less punishment as is in this Act mentioned.

44. False answers on enrolment.—Any person having become subject to this Act who is discovered to have made at the time of enrolment a wilfully false answer to any question set forth in the prescribed form of enrolment which has been put to him by the enrolling officer before whom he appears for the purpose of being enrolled shall, on conviction by court-martial, be liable to suffer imprisonment for a term which may extend to five years or such less punishment as is in this Act mentioned.

45. Unbecoming conduct.—Any officer, junior commissioned officer or warrant officer who behaves in a manner unbecoming his position and the character expected of him shall, on conviction by court-martial, if he is an officer, be liable to be cashiered or to suffer such less punishment as is in this Act mentioned; and, if he is a junior commissioned officer or a warrant officer, be liable to be dismissed or to suffer such less punishment as is in this Act mentioned.

46. Certain forms of disgraceful conduct.—Any person subject to this Act who commits any of the following offences, that is to say,—

(a) is guilty of any disgraceful conduct of a cruel, indecent or unnatural kinds; or

(b) malingers, or feigns, or produces disease or infirmity in himself, or intentionally delays his cure or aggravates his disease of infirmity; or

(c) with intent to render himself or any other person unfit for service, voluntarily causes hurt to himself or that person,

shall, on conviction by court-martial, be liable to suffer imprisonment for a term which may extend to seven years or such less punishment as is in this Act mentioned.

47. Ill-treating a subordinate.—Any officer, junior commissioned officer, warrant officer or non-commissioned officer who uses criminal force to or otherwise ill-treats any person subject to this Act, being his subordinate in rank or position, shall, on conviction by court-martial, be liable to suffer imprisonment for a term which may extend to seven years or such less punishment as is in this Act mentioned.

48. Intoxication.—(1) Any person subject to this Act who is found in a state of intoxication, whether on duty or not, shall, on conviction by court-martial, if he is an officer, be liable to be cashiered or to suffer such less punishment as is in this Act mentioned; and, if he is not an officer, be liable, subject to the provisions of sub-section (2), to suffer imprisonment for a term which may extend to two years or such less punishment as is in this Act mentioned.

(2) Where an offence of being intoxicated is committed by a person other than an officer when not on active service or not on duty, the period of imprisonment awarded shall not exceed six months.

49. Permitting escape of person in custody.—Any person subject to this Act who commits any of the following offences, that is to say,—

(a) when in command of a guard, picquet, patrol or post, releases without proper authority, whether wilfully or without reasonable excuse, any person committed to his charge, or refuses to receive any prisoner or person so committed; or

(b) wilfully or without reasonable excuse allows to escape any person who is committed to his charge, or whom it is his duty to keep or guard,

shall, on conviction by court-martial, be liable, if he has acted wilfully to suffer imprisonment for a term which may extend to fourteen years or such less punishment as is in this Act mentioned; and if he has not acted wilfully, to suffer imprisonment for a term which may extend to two years or such less punishment as is in this Act mentioned.

50. Irregularity in connection with arrest or confinement.—Any person subject to this Act who commits any of the following offences, that is to say,—

(a) unnecessarily detains a person in arrest or confinement without bringing him to trial, or fails to bring his case before the proper authority for investigation; or

(b) having committed a person to military custody fails without reasonable cause to deliver at the time of such committal, or as soon as practicable, and in any case within forty-eight hours thereafter, to the officer or other person into whose custody the person arrested is committed, an account in writing signed by himself of the offence with which the person so committed is charged,

shall, on conviction by court-martial, be liable to suffer imprisonment for a term which may extend to two years or such less punishment as is in this Act mentioned.

51. Escape from custody.—Any person subject to this Act who, being in lawful custody, escapes or attempts to escape, shall, on conviction by court-martial, be liable to suffer imprisonment for a term which may extend to five years or such less punishment as is in this Act mentioned.

52. Offences in respect of property.—Any person subject to this Act who commits any of the following offences, that is to say,—

(a) commits theft of any property belonging to the Government, or to any military, naval or air force mess, band or institution, or to any person subject to military, naval or air force law; or

(b) dishonestly misappropriates or converts to his own use any such property; or

(c) commits criminal breach of trust in respect of any such property; or

(d) dishonestly receives or retains any such property in respect of which any of the offences under clauses (a), (b) and (c) has been committed, knowing or having reason to believe the commission of such offence; or

(e) wilfully destroys or injures any property of the Government entrusted to him; or

(f) does any other thing with intent to defraud, or to cause wrongful gain to one person or wrongful loss to another person,

shall, on conviction by court-martial, be liable to suffer imprisonment for a term which may extend to ten years or such less punishment as is in this Act mentioned.

53. Extortion and corruption.—Any person subject to this Act who commits any of the following offences, that is to say,—

(a) commits extortion; or

(b) without proper authority exacts from any person money, provisions or service,

shall, on conviction by court-martial, be liable to suffer imprisonment for a term which may extend to ten years or such less punishment as is in this Act mentioned.

54. Making away with equipment.—Any person subject to this Act who commits any of the following offences, that is to say,—

(a) makes away with, or is concerned in making away with, any arms, ammunition, equipment, instruments, tools, clothing or any other thing being the property of the Government issued to him for his use or entrusted to him; or

(b) loses by neglect anything mentioned in clause (a); or

(c) sells, pawns, destroys or defaces any medal or decoration granted to him,

shall, on conviction by court-martial, be liable to suffer imprisonment for a term which may extend in the case of the offences specified in clause (a) to ten years, and in the case of the offences specified in the other clauses to five years, or such less punishment as is in this Act mentioned.

55. Injury to property.—Any person subject to this Act who commits any of the following offences, that is to say,—

(a) destroys or injures any property mentioned in clause (a) of section 54 or any property belonging to any military, naval or air force mess, band or institution, or to any person subject to military, naval or air force law, or serving with, or attached to, the regular Army; or

(b) commits any act which causes damage to, or destruction of, any property of the Government by fire; or

(c) kills, injures, makes away with, ill-treats or loses any animal entrusted to him,

shall, on conviction by court-martial, be liable, if he has acted wilfully, to suffer imprisonment for a term which may extend to fourteen years or such less punishment as is in this Act mentioned; and if he has acted without reasonable excuse, to suffer imprisonment for a term which may extend to seven years or such less punishment as is in this Act mentioned.

56. False accusations.—Any person subject to this Act who commits any of the following offences, that is to say,—

(a) makes a false accusation against any person subject to this Act, knowing or having reason to believe such accusation to be false; or

(b) in making a complaint under section 26 or section 27 makes any statement affecting the character of any person subject to this Act, knowing or having reason to believe such statement to be false or knowingly and wilfully suppresses any material facts,

shall, on conviction by court-martial, be liable to suffer imprisonment for a term which may extend to five years or such less punishment as is in this Act mentioned.

57. Falsifying official documents and false declaration.—Any person subject to this Act who commits any of the following offences, that is to say,—

(a) in any report, return, list, certificate, book or other document made or signed by him, or of the contents of which it is his duty to ascertain the accuracy, knowingly makes, or is privy to the making of any false or fraudulent statement; or

(b) in any document of the description mentioned in clause (a) knowingly makes, or is privy to the making of, any omission, with intent to defraud; or

(c) knowingly and with intent to injure any person, or knowingly and with intent to defraud, suppresses, defaces, alters or makes away with any documents which it is his duty to preserve or produce; or

(d) where it is his official duty to make a declaration respecting any matter, knowingly makes a false declaration; or

(e) obtains for himself, or for any other person, any pension, allowance or other advantage or privilege by a statement which is false, and which he either knows or believes to be false or does not believe to be true, or by making or using a false entry in any book or record or by making any document containing a false statement, or by omitting to make a true entry or document containing a true statement,

shall, on conviction by court-martial, be liable to suffer imprisonment for a term which may extend to fourteen years or such less punishment as is in this Act mentioned.

58. Signing in blank and failure to report.—Any person subject to this Act who commits any of the following offences, that is to say,—

(a) when signing any document relating to pay, arms, ammunition, equipment, clothing, supplies or stores, or any property or the Government fraudulently leaves in blank any material part for which his signature is a voucher; or

(b) refuses or by culpable neglect omits to make or send a report or return which it is his duty to make or send,

shall, on conviction by court-martial, be liable to suffer imprisonment for a term which may extend to seven years or such less punishment as is in this Act mentioned.

59. Offences relating to courts-martial.—Any person subject to this Act who commits any of the following offences, that is to say —

(a) being duly summoned or ordered to attend as a witness before a court-martial, wilfully or without reasonable excuse, makes default in attending; or

(b) refuses to take an oath or make an affirmation legally required by a court-martial to be taken or made; or

(c) refuses to produce or deliver any document in his power or control legally required by a court-martial to be produced or delivered by him; or

(d) refuses when a witness to answer any question which he is by law bound to answer; or

(e) is guilty of contempt of court-martial by using insulting or threatening language, or by causing any interruption or disturbance in the proceedings of such court,

shall, on conviction by court-martial, be liable to suffer imprisonment for a term which may extend to three years or such less punishment as is in this Act mentioned.

60. False evidence.—Any person subject to this Act who, having been duly sworn or affirmed before any court-martial or other court competent under this Act to administer an oath or affirmation, makes any statement which is false, and which he either knows or believes to be false or does not believe to be true, shall, on conviction by court-martial, be liable to suffer imprisonment for a term which may extend to seven years or such less punishment as is in this Act mentioned.

61. Unlawful detention of pay.—Any officer, junior commissioned officer, warrant officer or non-commissioned officer who, having received the pay of a person subject to this Act unlawfully detains or refuses to pay the same when due, shall, on conviction by court-martial, be liable to suffer imprisonment for a term which may extend to ten years or such less punishment as is in this Act mentioned.

62. Offences in relation to aircraft and flying.—Any person subject to this Act who commits any of the following offences, that is to say,—

(a) wilfully or without reasonable excuse damages, destroys or loses any aircraft or aircraft material belonging to the Government; or

(b) is guilty of any act or neglect likely to cause such damage, destruction or loss; or

(c) without lawful authority disposes of any aircraft or aircraft material belonging to the Government; or

(d) is guilty of any act or neglect in flying, or in the use of any aircraft, or in relation to any aircraft or aircraft material, which causes or is likely to cause loss of life or bodily injury to any person; or

(e) during a state of war, wilfully and without proper occasion, or negligently, causes the sequestration, by or under the authority of a neutral state, or the destruction in a neutral state or any aircraft belonging to the Government,

shall, on conviction by court-martial, be liable, if he has acted wilfully, to suffer imprisonment for a term which may extend to fourteen years or such less punishment as is in this Act mentioned, and, in any other case, to suffer imprisonment for a term which may extend to five years or such less punishment as is in this Act mentioned.

63. Violation of good order and discipline.—Any person subject to this Act who is guilty of any act or omission which, though not specified in this Act, is prejudicial to good order and military discipline shall, on conviction by court-martial, be liable to suffer imprisonment for a term which may extend to seven years of such less punishment as is in this Act mentioned.

COMMENTS

If an offence is covered under section 63, while awarding the punishment the court-martial has to keep in view the spirit behind section 72 of the Act and it has to give due regard to the nature and degree of the offence; *Ex-Naik Sardar Singh* v. *Union of India*, AIR 1992 SC 417.

64. Miscellaneous offences.—Any person subject to this Act who commits any of the following offences, that is to say,—

(a) being in command at any post or on the march, and receiving a complaint that any one under his command has beaten or otherwise maltreated or oppressed any person, or has disturbed any fair or market, or committed any riot or trespass, fails to have due reparation made to the injured person or to report the case to the proper authority; or

(b) by defiling any place of worship, or otherwise, intentionally insults the religion or wounds the religious feelings of any person; or

(c) attempts to commit suicide, and in such attempt does any act towards the commission of such offence; or

(d) being below the rank of warrant officer, when off duty, appears, without proper authority, in or about camp or cantonments, or in or about, or when going to or returning from any town or bazar, carrying a rifle, sword or other offensive weapon; or

(e) directly or indirectly accepts or obtains, or agrees to accept or attempts to obtain, for himself or for any other person, any gratification as a motive or reward for procuring the enrolment of any person, or leave of absence, promotion or any other advantage or indulgence for any person in the service; or

(f) commits any offence against the property or person of any inhabitant of, or resident in, the country in which he is serving,

shall, on conviction by court-martial, be liable to suffer imprisonment for a term which may extend to seven years or such less punishment as is in this Act mentioned.

65. Attempt.—Any person subject to this Act who attempts to commit any of the offences specified in sections 34 to 64 inclusive and in such attempt does any act towards the commission of the offence, shall, on conviction by court-martial, where no express provision is made by this Act for the punishment of such attempt, be liable,

if the offence attempted to be committed is punishable with death, to suffer imprisonment for a term which may extend to fourteen years or such less punishment as is in this Act mentioned; and

if the offence attempted to be committed is punishable with imprisonment, to suffer imprisonment for a term which may extend to one-half of the longest term provided for that offence or such less punishment as is in this Act mentioned.

66. Abetment of offences that have been committed.—Any person subject to this Act who abets the commission of any of the offences specified in sections 34 to 64 inclusive shall, on conviction by court-martial, if the Act abetted is committed in consequence of the abetment and no express provision is made by this Act for the punishment of such abetment, be liable to suffer the punishment provided for that offence or such less punishment as is in this Act mentioned.

67. Abetment of offences punishable with death and not committed.—Any person subject to this Act who abets the commission of any of the offences punishable with death under sections 34, 37 and sub-section (1) of section 38, shall, on conviction by court-martial, if that offence be not committed in consequence of the abetment, and no express provision is made by this Act for the punishment of such abetment, be liable to suffer imprisonment for a term which may extend to fourteen years or such less punishment as is in this Act mentioned.

68. Abetment of offences punishable with imprisonment and not committed.—Any person subject to this Act who abets the commission of any of the offences specified in sections 34 to 64 inclusive and punishable with imprisonment shall, on conviction by court-martial, if that offence be not committed in consequence of the abetment, and no express provision is made by this Act for the punishment of such abetment, be liable to suffer imprisonment for a term which may extend to one-half of the longest term provided for that offence or such less punishment as is in this Act mentioned.

69. Civil offences.—Subject to the provisions of section 70, any person subject to this Act who at any place in or beyond India, commits any civil offence, shall be deemed to be guilty of an offence against this Act and, if charged therewith under this section, shall be liable to be tried by a court-martial and, on conviction, be punishable as follows, that is to say,—

(a) if the offence is one which would be punishable under any law in force in India with death or with transportation, he shall be liable to suffer any punishment, other than whipping, assigned for the offence, by the aforesaid law and such less punishment as is in this Act mentioned; and

(b) in any other case, he shall be liable to suffer any punishment, other than whipping, assigned for the offence by the law in force in India, or imprisonment for a term which may extend to seven years, or such less punishment as is in this Act mentioned.

70. Civil offences not triable by court-martial.—A person subject to this Act who commits an offence of murder against a person not subject to military, naval or air force law, or of culpable homicide not amounting to murder against such a person or of rape in relation to such a person, shall not be deemed to be guilty of an offence against this Act and shall not be tried by a court-martial, unless he commits any of the said offences—

(a) while on active service, or

(b) at any place outside India, or

(c) at a frontier post specified by the Central Government by notification in this behalf.

[1][***]

CHAPTER VII

PUNISHMENTS

71. Punishments awardable by courts-martial.—Punishments may be inflicted in respect of offences committed by persons subject to this Act and convicted by courts-martial, according to the scale following, that is to say,—

(a) death;

(b) transportation for life or for any period not less than seven years;

(c) imprisonment either rigorous or simple, for any period not exceeding fourteen years;

(d) cashiering, in the case of officers;

(e) dismissal from the service;

(f) reduction to the ranks or to a lower rank or grade or place in the list of their rank, in the case of warrant officers; and reduction to the ranks or to a lower rank or grade, in the case of non-commissioned officers:

Provided that a warrant officer reduced to the ranks shall not be required to serve in the ranks as a sepoy;

(g) forfeiture of seniority of rank, in the case of officers, junior commissioned officers, warrant officers and non-commissioned officers; and forfeiture of all or any part of their service for the purpose of promotion, in the case of any of them whose promotion depends upon length of service;

---

1. *Explanation* omitted by Act 13 of 1975, sec. 4.

(h) forfeiture of service for the purpose of increased pay pension or any other prescribed purpose;

(i) severe reprimand or reprimand, in the case of officers, junior commissioned officers, warrant officers and non-commissioned officers;

(j) forfeiture of pay and allowances for a period not exceeding three months for an offence committed on active service;

(k) forfeiture in the case of a person sentenced to cashiering or dismissal from the service of all arrears of pay and allowances and other public money due to him at the time of such cashiering or dismissal;

(l) stoppage of pay and allowances until any proved loss or damage occasioned by the offence of which he is convicted is made good.

72. Alternative punishments awardable by court-martial.—Subject to the provisions of this Act, a court-martial may, on convicting a person subject to this Act of any of the offences specified in sections 34 to 68 inclusive, award either the particular punishment with which the offence is stated in the said sections to be punishable, or, in lieu thereof, any one of the punishments lower in the scale set out in section 71, regard being had to the nature and degree of the offence.

73. Combination of punishments.—A sentence of a court-martial may award in addition to, or without any one other punishment, the punishment specified in clause (d) or clause (e) of section 71 and any one or more of the punishments specified in clauses (f) to (l) of that section.

74. Cashiering of officers.—An officer shall be sentenced to be cashiered before he is awarded any of the punishments specified in clauses (a) to (c) of section 71.

75. Field punishment.—[*Rep. by the Army (Amendment) Act, 1992 (37 of 1992), sec. 2 (w.e.f. 6-9-1992).*]

76. Position of field punishment in scale of punishment.—[*Rep. by the Army (Amendment) Act, 1992 (37 of 1992), sec. 2 (w.e.f. 6-9-1992).*]

77. Result of certain punishments in the case of a warrant officer or non-commissioned officer.—A warrant officer or a non-commissioned officer sentenced by a court-martial to transportation, imprisonment [1][***] or dismissal from the service, shall be deemed to be reduced to the ranks.

78. Retention in the ranks of a person convicted on active service.—When, on active service, any enrolled person has been sentenced by a court-martial to dismissal, or to transportation or imprisonment whether combined with dismissal or not, the prescribed officer may direct that such person may be retained to serve in the ranks, and such service shall be reckoned as part of his term of transportation or imprisonment, if any.

79. Punishments otherwise than by court-martial.—Punishments may also be inflicted in respect of offences committed by persons subject to this Act without the intervention of a court-martial and in the manner stated in sections 80, 83, 84 and 85.

80. Punishment of persons other than officers, junior commissioned officers and warrant officers.—Subject to the provisions of section 81, a commanding officer or such other officer as is, with the consent of the Central Government, specified by [2][the Chief of the Army Staff], may, in the prescribed manner, proceed against a person subject to this Act otherwise than as an officer, junior commissioned officer or warrant officer who is charged with an offence under this Act and award such person, to the extent prescribed, one or more of the following punishments, that is to say,—

(a) imprisonment in military custody up to twenty-eight days;

(b) detention up to twenty-eight days;

(c) confinement to the lines upto twenty-eight days;

(d) extra guards or duties;

(e) deprivation of a position of the nature of an appointment or of corps or working pay, and in the case of non-commissioned officers, also deprivation of acting rank or reduction to a lower grade of pay;

(f) forfeiture of good service and good conduct pay;

---

1. The words "field punishment" omitted by Act 37 of 1992, sec. 3 (w.e.f. 6-9-1992).

2. Subs. by Act 19 of 1955, sec. 2 and Sch., for "the Commander-in-Chief".

(g) severe reprimand or reprimand;

(h) fine up to fourteen days' pay in any one month;

(i) penal deductions under clause (g) of section 91;

[1][***]

81. Limit of punishments under section 80.—[2][***]

(2) In the case of an award of two or more of the punishments specified in clauses (a), (b), (c) and (d) of the said section, the punishment specified in clause (c) or clause (d) shall take effect only at the end of the punishment specified in clause (a) or clause (b).

(3) When two or more of the punishments specified in the said clauses (a), (b) and (c) are awarded to a person conjointly, or when already undergoing one or more of the said punishments, the whole extent of the punishments shall not exceed in the aggregate forty-two days.

(4) The punishments specified in clauses [3][(a), (b) and (c)] of section 80 shall not be awarded to any person who is of the rank of non-commissioned officer or was, at the time of committing the offence for which he is punished, of such rank.

(5) The punishment specified in clause (g) of the said section shall not be awarded to any person below the rank of a non-commissioned officer.

82. Punishments in addition to those specified in section 80.—[4][The Chief of the Army Staff] may, with the consent of the Central Government, specify such other punishments as may be awarded under section 80 in addition to or without any of the punishments specified in the said section, and the extent to which such other punishments may be awarded.

83. Punishment of officers, junior commissioned officers and warrant officers by brigade commanders and others.—An officer having power not less than a brigade, or an equivalent

---

1. Clause (j) omitted by Act 37 of 1992, sec. 4 (w.e.f. 6-9-1992).
2. Sub-section (1) omitted by Act 37 of 1992, sec. 5 (w.e.f. 6-9-1992).
3. Subs. by Act 37 of 1992, sec. 5, for "(a), (b), (c) and (j)" (w.e.f. 6-9-1992).
4. Subs. by Act 19 of 1955, sec. 2 and Sch., for "the Commander-in-Chief".

commander or such other officer as is, with the consent of the Central Government specified by [1][the Chief of the Army Staff] may, in the prescribed manner, proceed against an officer below the rank of a field officer, a junior commissioned officer or a warrant officer, who is charged with an offence under this Act, and award one or more of the following punishments, that is to say,—

(a) severe reprimand or reprimand;

(b) stoppage of pay and allowances until any proved loss or damage occasioned by the offence of which he is convicted is made good.

84. Punishment of officers, junior commissioned officers and warrant officers by area commanders and others.—An officer having power not less than an area commander or an equivalent commander or an officer empowered to convene a general court-martial or such other officer as is, with the consent of the Central Government, specified by [1][the Chief of the Army Staff] may, in the prescribed manner, proceed against an officer below the rank of lieutenant-colonel, a junior commissioned officer or a warrant officer, who is charged with an offence under this Act, and award one or more of the following punishments, that is to say,—

(a) forfeiture of seniority, or in the case of any of them whose promotion depends upon length of service, forfeiture of service for the purpose of promotion for a period not exceeding twelve months, but subject to the right of the accused previous to the award to elect to be tried by a court-martial;

(b) severe reprimand or reprimand;

(c) stoppage of pay and allowances until any proved loss or damage occasioned by the offence of which he is convicted is made good.

85. Punishment of junior commissioned officers.—A commanding officer or such other officer as is, with the consent of the Central Government, specified by [1][the Chief of the Army Staff], may, in the prescribed manner, proceed against a junior

1. Subs. by Act 19 of 1955, sec. 2 and Sch., for "the Commander-in-Chief".

commissioned officer who is charged with an offence under this Act. [1][and award one or more of the following punishments, that is to say,—

(i) severe reprimand or reprimand;

(ii) stoppage of pay and allowances until any proved loss or damage occasioned by the offence of which he is convicted is made good:

Provided that the punishment specified in clause (i) shall not be awarded if the commanding officer or such other officer is below the rank of Colonel.]

86. Transmission of proceedings.—In every case in which punishment has been awarded under any of the sections 83, 84 and 85, certified true copies of the proceedings shall be forwarded, in the prescribed manner, by the officer awarding the punishment, to a superior military authority as defined in section 88.

87. Review of proceedings.—If any punishment awarded under any of the sections 83, 84 and 85 appears to a superior military authority as defined in section 88 to be illegal, unjust or excessive, such authority may cancel, vary or remit the punishment and make such other direction as may be appropriate in the circumstances of the case.

88. Superior military authority.—For the purpose of sections 86 and 87, a "superior military authority" means—

(a) in the case of punishments awarded by a commanding officer, any officer superior in command to such commanding officer;

(b) in the case of punishments awarded by any other authority, the Central Government, [2][the Chief of the Army Staff] or other officer specified by [2][the Chief of the Army Staff].

89. Collective fines.—(1) Whenever any weapon or part of a weapon forming part of the equipment of a half squadron, battery, company or other similar unit is lost or stolen, the officer commanding the army, army corps, division or independent

1. Subs. by Act 37 of 1992, sec. 6, for certain words (w.e.f. 6-9-1992).
2. Subs. by Act 19 of 1955, sec. 2 and Sch., for "the Commander-in-Chief".

brigade to which such unit belongs may, after obtaining the report of a court of inquiry, impose a collective fine upon the junior commissioned officers, warrant officers, non-commissioned officers and men of such unit, or upon so many of them as, in his judgment, should be held responsible for such loss or theft.

(2) Such fine shall be assessed as a percentage on the pay of the individuals on whom it falls.

CHAPTER VIII

PENAL DEDUCTIONS

90. Deductions from pay and allowances of officers.—The following penal deductions may be made from the pay and allowances of an officer, that is to say,—

(a) all pay and allowances due to an officer for every day he absents himself without leave, unless a satisfactory explanation has been given to his commanding officer and has been approved by the Central Government;

(b) all pay and allowances for every day while he is in custody or under suspension from duty on a charge for an offence for which he is afterwards convicted by a criminal court or a court-martial or by an officer exercising authority under section 83 or section 84;

(c) any sum required to make good the pay of any person subject to this Act which he has unlawfully retained or unlawfully refused to pay;

(d) any sum required to make good such compensation for any expenses, loss, damage or destruction occasioned by the commission of an offence as may be determined by the court-martial by whom he is convicted of such offence, or by an officer exercising authority under section 83 or section 84;

(e) all pay and allowances ordered by a court-martial [1][***] to be forfeited or stopped;

(f) any sum required to pay a fine awarded by a criminal court or a court-martial exercising jurisdiction under section 69;

---

1. The words "or an officer exercising authority under section 85" omitted by Act 37 of 1992, sec. 7 (w.e.f. 6-9-1992).

(g) any sum required to make good any loss, damage, or destruction of public or regimental property which, after due investigation, appears to the Central Government to have been occasioned by the wrongful act or negligence on the part of the officer;

(h) all pay and allowances forfeited by order of the Central Government if the officer is found by a court of inquiry constituted by [1][the Chief of the Army Staff] in this behalf, to have deserted to the enemy, or while in enemy hands, to have served with, or under the orders of, the enemy, or in any manner to have aided the enemy, or to have allowed himself to be taken prisoner by the enemy through want of due precaution or through disobedience of orders or wilful neglect of duty, or having been taken prisoner by the enemy, to have failed to rejoin his service when it was possible to do so;

(i) any sum required by order of the Central Government [2][or any prescribed officer] to be paid for the maintenance of his wife or his legitimate or illegitimate child or towards the cost of any relief given by the said Government to the said wife or child.

91. Deductions from pay and allowances of persons other than officers.—Subject to the provisions of section 94 the following penal deductions may be made from the pay and allowances of a person subject to this Act other than an officer, that is to say,—

(a) all pay and allowances for every day of absence either on desertion or without leave, or as a prisoner of war, and for every day of transportation or imprisonment awarded by a criminal court, a court-martial or an officer exercising authority under section 80, [3][***];

(b) all pay and allowances for every day while he is in custody on a charge for an offence of which he is afterwards

---

1. Subs. by Act 19 of 1955, sec. 2 and Sch., for "the Commander-in-Chief".
2. Ins. by Act 37 of 1992, sec. 7 (w.e.f. 6-9-1992).
3. The words "or of field punishment awarded by a court-martial or such officer" omitted by Act 37 of 1992, sec. 8 (w.e.f. 6-9-1992).

convicted by a criminal court or a court-martial, or on a charge of absence without leave for which he is afterwards awarded imprisonment [1][***] by an officer exercising authority under section 80;

(c) all pay and allowances for every day on which he is in hospital on account of sickness certified by the medical officer attending on him to have been caused by an offence under this Act committed by him;

(d) for every day on which he is in hospital on account of sickness certified by the medical officer attending on him to have been caused by his own misconduct or imprudence, such sum as may be specified by order of the Central Government or such officer as may be specified by that Government;

(e) all pay and allowances ordered by a court-martial or by an officer exercising authority under any of the sections 80, 83, 84 and 85, to be forfeited or stopped;

(f) all pay and allowances for every day between his being recovered from the enemy and his dismissal from the service in consequence of his conduct when being taken prisoner by, or while in the hands of, the enemy;

(g) any sum required to make good such compensation for any expenses, loss, damage or destruction caused by him to the Central Government or to any building or property as may be awarded by his commanding officer;

(h) any sum required to pay a fine awarded by a criminal court, a court-martial exercising jurisdiction under section 69, or an officer exercising authority under any of the sections 80 and 89;

(i) any sum required by order of the Central Government or any prescribed officer to be paid for the maintenance of his wife or his legitimate or illegitimate child or towards the cost of any relief given by the said Government to the said wife or child.

92. Computation of time of absence or custody.—For the purposes of clauses (a) and (b) of section 91,—

1. The words "or field punishment" omitted by Act 37 of 1992, sec. 8 (w.e.f. 6-9-1992).

(a) no person shall be treated as absent or in custody for a day unless the absence or custody has lasted, whether wholly in one day, or partly in one day and partly in another, for six consecutive hours or upwards;

(b) any absence or custody for less than a day may be reckoned as absence or custody for a day if such absence or custody prevented the absentee from fulfilling any military duty which was thereby thrown upon some other person;

(c) absence or custody for twelve consecutive hours or upwards may be reckoned as absence or custody for the whole of each day during any portion of which the person was absent or in custody;

(d) a period of absence, or imprisonment, which commences before, and ends after, midnight, may be reckoned as a day.

93. Pay and allowances during trial.—In the case of any person subject to this Act who is in custody or under suspension from duty on a charge for an offence, the prescribed officer may direct that the whole or any part of the pay and allowances of such person shall be withheld, pending the result of his trial on the charge against him, in order to give effect to the provisions of clause (b) of sections 90 and 91.

94. Limit of certain deductions.—The total deductions from the pay and allowances of a person made under clauses (e), (g) to (i) of section 91 shall not, except where he is sentenced to dismissal, exceed in any one month one-half of his pay and allowances for that month.

95. Deduction from public money due to a person.—Any sum authorised by this Act to be deducted from the pay and allowances of any person may, without prejudice to any other mode of recovering the same, be deducted from any public money due to him other than a pension.

96. Pay and allowances of prisoner of war during inquiry into his conduct.—Where the conduct of any person subject to this Act when being taken prisoner by, or while in the hands of, the enemy, is to be inquired into under this Act or any other law, [1][the Chief of the Army Staff] or any officer authorised by him may order that the

1. Subs. by Act 19 of 1955, sec. 2 and Sch., for "the Commander-in-Chief".

whole or any part of the pay and allowances of such person shall be withheld pending the result of such inquiry.

97. Remission of deductions.—Any deduction from pay and allowances authorised by this Act may be remitted in such manner and to such extent, and by such authority, as may from time-to-time be prescribed.

98. Provision for dependants of prisoner of war from remitted deductions.—In the case of all persons subject to this Act, being prisoners of war, whose pay and allowances have been forfeited under clause (h) of section 90 or clause (a) of section 91, but in respect of whom a remission has been made under section 97, it shall be lawful for proper provision to be made by the prescribed authorities out of such pay and allowances for any dependants of such persons, and any such remission shall in that case be deemed to apply only to the balance thereafter remaining of such pay and allowances.

99. Provision for dependants of prisoner of war from his pay and allowances.—It shall be lawful for proper provision to be made by the prescribed authorities for any dependants of any person subject to this Act who is a prisoner of war or is missing, out of his pay and allowances.

100. Period during which a person is deemed to be a prisoner of war.—For the purposes of sections 98 and 99, a person shall be deemed to continue to be a prisoner of war until the conclusion of any inquiry into his conduct such as is referred to in section 96, and if he is cashiered or dismissed from the service in consequence of such conduct, until the date of such cashiering or dismissal.

CHAPTER IX

ARREST AND PROCEEDINGS BEFORE TRIAL

101. Custody of offenders.—(1) Any person subject to this Act who is charged with an offence may be taken into military custody.

(2) Any such person may be ordered into military custody by any superior officer.

(3) An officer may order into military custody any officer, though he may be of higher rank, engaged in a quarrel, affray or disorder.

102. Duty of commanding officer in regard to detention.—(1) It shall be the duty of every commanding officer to take care that a person under his command when charged with an offence is not detained in custody for more than forty-eight hours after the committal of such person into custody is reported to him, without the charge being investigated, unless investigation within that period seems to him to be impracticable having regard to the public service.

(2) The case of every person being detained in custody beyond a period of forty-eight hours, and the reason thereof, shall be reported by the Commanding Officer to the General or other officer to whom application would be made to convene a general or district court-martial for the trial of the person charged.

(3) In reckoning the period of forty-eight hours specified in sub-section (1), Sundays and other public holidays shall be excluded.

(4) Subject to the provisions of this Act, the Central Government may make rules providing for the manner in which and the period for which any person subject to this Act may be taken into and detained in military custody, pending the trial by any competent authority for any offence committed by him.

103. Interval between committal and court-martial.—In every case where any such person as is mentioned in section 101 and as is not on active service remains in such custody for a longer period than eight days, without a court-martial for his trial being ordered to assemble, a special report giving reasons for the delay shall be made by his commanding officer in the manner prescribed, and a similar report shall be forwarded at intervals of every eight days until a court-martial is assembled or such person is released from custody.

104. Arrest by civil authorities.—Wherever any person subject to this Act, who is accused of any offence under this Act, is within the jurisdiction of any magistrate or police officer, such magistrate or police officer shall aid in the apprehension and delivery to military custody of such person upon receipt of a written application to that effect signed by his commanding officer.

105. Capture of deserters.—(1) Whenever any person subject to this Act deserts, the commanding officer of the corps, department or detachment to which he belongs, shall give written information of the desertion to such civil authorities as, in his opinion, may be able to afford assistance towards the capture of the deserter; and such authorities shall thereupon take steps for the apprehension of the said deserter in like manner as if he were a person for whose apprehension a warrant had been issued by a magistrate, and shall deliver the deserter, when apprehended, into military custody.

(2) Any police officer may arrest without warrant any person reasonably believed to be subject to this Act, and to be a deserter or to be travelling without authority, and shall bring him without delay before the nearest magistrate, to be dealt with according to law.

106. Inquiry into absence without leave.—(1) When any person subject to this Act has been absent from his duty without due authority for a period of thirty days, a court of inquiry shall, as soon as practicable, be assembled, and such court shall, on oath or affirmation administered in the prescribed manner, inquire respecting the absence of the person, and the deficiency, if any, in the property of the Government entrusted to his care, or in any arms, ammunition, equipment, instruments, clothing or necessaries; and if satisfied of the fact of such absence without due authority or other sufficient cause, the court shall declare such absence and the period thereof, and the said deficiency, if any, and the commanding officer of the corps or department to which the person belongs shall enter in the court-martial book of the corps or department a record of the declaration.

(2) If the person declared absent does not afterwards surrender or is not apprehended, he shall, for the purposes of this Act, be deemed to be a deserter.

107. Provost-marshals.—(1) Provost-marshals may be appointed by [1][the Chief of the Army Staff] or by any prescribed officer.

(2) The duties of a provost-marshal are to take charge of persons confined for any offence, to preserve good order and discipline, and to prevent breaches of the same by persons serving in, or attached to, the regular Army.

---

1. Subs. by Act 19 of 1955, sec. 2 and Sch., for "the Commander-in-Chief".

(3) A provost-marshal may at any time arrest and detain for trial any person subject to this Act who commits, or is charged with an offence, and may also carry into effect any punishment to be inflicted in pursuance of the sentence awarded by a court-martial, or by an officer exercising authority under section 80 but shall not inflict any punishment on his own authority:

Provided that no officer shall be so arrested or detained otherwise than on the order of another officer.

(4) For the purposes of sub-sections (2) and (3), a provost-marshal shall be deemed to include a provost-marshal appointed under any law for the time being in force relating to the Government of the Navy or Air Force, and any person legally exercising authority under him or on his behalf.

CHAPTER X

COURTS-MARTIAL

108. Kinds of courts-martial.—For the purposes of this Act there shall be four kinds of courts-martial, that is to say,—

(a) general courts-martial;

(b) district courts-martial;

(c) summary general courts-martial; and

(d) summary courts-martial.

109. Power to convene a general court-martial.—A general court-martial may be convened by the Central Government of [1][the Chief of the Army Staff] or by any officer empowered in this behalf by warrant of [1][the Chief of the Army Staff].

COMMENTS

There is nothing in section 109 of the Act which requires the Chief of the Army Staff to issue a warrant for each specific case. A general warrant issued by the Chief of the Army Staff is competent under section 109; *Major General Inder Jit Kumar* v. *Union of India*, AIR 1997 SC 2085.

110. Power to convene a district court-martial.—A district court-martial may be convened by an officer having power to

---

1. Subs. by Act 19 of 1955, sec. 2 and Sch., for "the Commander-in-Chief".

convene a general court-martial or by officer empowered in this behalf by warrant of any such officer.

111. Contents of warrants issued under sections 109 and 110.—A warrant issued under section 109 or section 110 may contain such restrictions, reservations or conditions as the officer issuing it may think fit.

112. Power to convene a summary general court-martial.—The following authorities shall have power to convene a summary general court-martial, namely:—

(a) an officer empowered in this behalf by an order of the Central Government or of [1][the Chief of the Army Staff];

(b) on active service, the officer commanding the forces in the field, or any officer empowered by him in this behalf;

(c) an officer commanding any detached portion of the regular Army on active service when, in his opinion, it is not practicable, with due regard to discipline and the exigencies of the service, that an offence should be tried by a general court-martial.

113. Composition of general court-martial.—A general court-martial shall consist of not less than five officers, each of whom has held a commission for not less than three whole years and of whom not less than four are of a rank not below that of captain.

114. Composition of district court-martial.—A district court-martial shall consist of not less than three officers, each of whom has held a commission for not less than two whole years.

115. Composition of summary general court-martial.—A summary general court-martial shall consist of not less than three officers.

116. Summary court-martial.—(1) A summary court-martial may be held by the commanding officer of any corps, department or detachment of the regular Army, and he shall alone constitute the court.

(2) The proceedings shall be attended throughout by two other persons who shall be officers or junior commissioned officers or one of either, and who shall not as such, be sworn or affirmed.

---

1. Subs. by Act 19 of 1955, sec. 2 and Sch., for "the Commander-in-Chief".

117. Dissolution of courts-martial.—(1) If a court-martial after the commencement of a trial reduced below the minimum number of officers required by this Act, it shall be dissolved.

(2) If, on account of the illness of the judge-advocate or of the accused before the finding, it is impossible to continue the trial, a court-martial shall be dissolved.

(3) The officer who convened a court-martial may dissolve such court-martial if it appears to him that military exigencies or the necessities of discipline render it impossible or inexpedient to continue the said court-martial.

(4) Where a court-martial is dissolved under this section, the accused may be tried again.

118. Powers of general and summary general courts-martial.—A general or summary general court-martial shall have power to try any person subject to this Act for any offence punishable therein and to pass any sentence authorised thereby.

119. Powers of district courts-martial.—A district court-martial shall have power to try any person subject to this Act other than an officer of a junior commissioned officer for any offence made punishable therein, and to pass any sentence authorised by this Act other than a sentence of death, transportation, or imprisonment for a term exceeding two years:

Provided that a district court-martial shall not sentence a warrant officer to imprisonment.

120. Powers of summary courts-martial.—(1) Subject to the provisions of sub-section (2), a summary court-martial may try any offence punishable under this Act.

(2) When there is no grave reason for immediate action and reference can without detriment to discipline be made to the officer empowered to convene a district court-martial or on active service a summary general court-martial for the trial of the alleged offender, an officer holding a summary court-martial shall not try without such reference any offence punishable under any of the sections 34, 37 and 69, or any offence against the officer holding the court.

(3) A summary court-martial may try any person subject to this Act and under the command of the officer holding the court, except an officer, junior commissioned officer or warrant officer.

(4) A summary court-martial may pass any sentence which may be passed under this Act, except a sentence of death or transportation, or of imprisonment for a term exceeding the limit specified in sub-section (5).

(5) The limit referred to in sub-section (4) shall be one year if the officer holding the summary court-martial is of the rank of lieutenant-colonel and upwards, and three months, if such officer is below that rank.

121. Prohibition of second trial.—When any person subject to this Act has been acquitted or convicted of an offence by a court-martial or by a criminal court, or has been dealt with under any of the sections 80, 83, 84 and 85, he shall not be liable to be tried again for the same offence by a court-martial or dealt with under the said sections.

COMMENTS

Where a member of the army staff, after authorities decided his trial by the court-martial, was neither convicted nor acquitted and was also not dealt with under section 80, 83, 84 or 85 of the Act, sending him to a regular criminal court for standing trial would not be prohibited; *Chief of Army Staff* v. *Major E.P. Chadha*, AIR 1991 SC 460.

122. Period of limitation for trial.—(1) Except as provided by sub-section (2), no trial by court-martial of any person subject to this Act for any offence shall be commenced after the expiration of a period of three years [1][and such period shall commence,—

(a) on the date of the offence; or

(b) where the commission of the offence was not known to the person aggrieved by the offence or to the authority competent to initiate action, the first day on which such offence comes to the knowledge of such person or authority, whichever is earlier; or

(c) where it is not known by whom the offence was committed, the first day on which the identity of the offender is known to the person aggrieved by the offence or to the authority competent to initiate action, whichever is earlier.]

1. Subs. by Act 37 of 1992, sec. 9, for "from the date of such offence" (w.e.f. 6-9-1992).

(2) The provisions of sub-section (1) shall not apply to a trial for an offence of desertion or fraudulent enrolment or for any of the offences mentioned in section 37.

(3) In the computation of the period of time mentioned in sub-section (1), any time spent by such person as a prisoner of war, or in enemy territory, or in evading arrest after the commission of the offence, shall be excluded.

(4) No trial for an offence of desertion other than desertion on active service or of fraudulent enrolment shall be commenced if the person in question, not being an officer, has subsequently to the commission of the offence, served continuously in an exemplary manner for not less than three years with any portion of the regular Army.

123. Liability of offender who ceases to be subject to Act.—(1) Where an offence under this Act had been committed by any person while subject to this Act, and he has ceased to be so subject, he may be taken into and kept in military custody, and tried and punished for such offence as if he continued to be so subject.

(2) No such persons shall be tried for an offence, unless his trial commences [1][within a period of three years after he had ceased to be subject to this Act; and in computing such period, the time during which such person has avoided arrest by absconding or concealing himself or where the institution of the proceeding in respect of the offence has been stayed by an injunction or order, the period of the continuance of the injunction or order, the day on which it was issued or made, and the day on which it was withdrawn, shall be excluded:]

Provided that nothing contained in this sub-section shall apply to the trial of any such person for an offence of desertion of fraudulent enrolment or for any of the offences mentioned in section 37 or shall affect the jurisdiction of a criminal court to try any offence triable by such court as well as by a court-martial.

(3) When a person subject to this Act is sentenced by a court-martial to transportation or imprisonment, this Act shall apply to him during the term of his sentence, though he is

1. Subs. by Act 37 of 1992, sec. 10, for "within six months after he had ceased to be subject to this Act" (w.e.f. 6-9-1992).

cashiered or dismissed from the regular Army, or has otherwise ceased to be subject to this Act, and he may be kept, removed, imprisoned and punished as if he continued to be subject to this Act.

(4) When a person subject to this Act is sentenced by a court-martial to death, this Act shall apply to him till the sentence is carried out.

COMMENTS

(i) An Army officer consequent upon his retirement, even though ceased to be subject to the Act, can be dismissed from service for committing an offence under the Act; *Union of India* v. *R.K.L.D. Azad,* AIR 1996 SC 845.

(ii) The trial commences the moment General Court-Martial assembles to consider the charge and examines whether they would proceed with the trial. The preceding preliminary investigation is only a part of the process of investigation to find whether a charge could be framed and placed before the competent authority to constitute General Court-Martial; *Union of India* v. *Major General Madan Lal Yadav,* AIR 1996 SC 1340.

124. Place of trial.—Any person subject to this Act who commits any offence against it may be tried and punished for such offence in any place whatever.

125. Choice between criminal court and court-martial.—When a criminal court and a court-martial have each jurisdiction in respect of an offence, it shall be in the discretion of the officer commanding the army, army corps, division or independent brigade in which the accused person is serving or such other officer as may be prescribed to decide before which court the proceedings shall be instituted, and, if that officer decides that they should be instituted before a court-martial, to direct that the accused person shall be detained in military custody.

126. Power of criminal court to require delivery of offender.—(1) When a criminal court having jurisdiction is of opinion that proceedings shall be instituted before itself in respect of any alleged offence, it may, by written notice, require the officer referred to in section 125 at his option, either to deliver over the offender to the nearest magistrate to be proceeded against according to law, or to postpone proceedings pending a reference to the Central Government.

(2) In every such case the said officer shall either deliver over the offender in compliance with the requisition, or shall forthwith refer the question as to the court before which the proceedings are to be instituted for the determination of the Central Government, whose order upon such reference shall be final.

[1][***]

CHAPTER XI

PROCEDURE OF COURTS-MARTIAL

128. Presiding officer.—At every general, district or summary general court-martial the senior member shall be the presiding officer.

129. Judge-advocate.—Every general court-martial shall, and every district or summary general court-martial may, be attended by a judge-advocate, who shall be either an officer belonging to the department of the Judge-Advocate General, or if no such officer is available, an officer approved of by the Judge-Advocate General or any of his deputies.

130. Challenges.—(1) At all trials by general, district or summary general court-martial, as soon as the court is assembled, the names of the presiding officer and members shall be read over to the accused, who shall thereupon be asked whether he objects to being tried by any officer sitting on the court.

(2) If the accused objects to any such officer, his objection, and also the reply thereto of the officer objected to, shall be heard and recorded and the remaining officers of the court shall, in the absence of the challenged officer decide on the objection.

(3) If the objection is allowed by one-half or more of the votes of the officers entitled to vote, the objection shall be allowed, and the member objected to shall retire, and his vacancy may be filled in the prescribed manner by another officer subject to the same right of the accused to object.

(4) When no challenge is made, or when challenge has been made and disallowed, or the place of every officer successfully challenged has been filled by another officer to whom no objection is made or allowed, the court shall proceed with the trial.

1. Section 127 omitted by Act 37 of 1992, sec. 11 (w.e.f. 6-9-1992).

131. Oaths of member, judge-advocate and witness.—(1) An oath or affirmation in the prescribed manner shall be administered to every member of every court-martial and to the judge-advocate before the commencement of the trial.

(2) Every person giving evidence before a court-martial shall be examined after being duly sworn or affirmed in the prescribed form.

(3) The provisions of sub-section (2) shall not apply where the witness is a child under twelve years of age and the court-martial is of opinion that though the witness understands the duty of speaking the truth, he does not understand the nature of an oath or affirmation.

132. Voting by members.—(1) Subject to the provisions of sub-sections (2) and (3), every decision of a court-martial shall be passed by an absolute majority of votes; and where there is an equality of votes on either the finding or the sentence, the decision shall be in favour of the accused.

(2) No sentence of death shall be passed by a general court-martial without the concurrence of at least two-thirds of the members of the court.

(3) No sentence of death shall be passed by a summary general court-martial without the concurrence of all the members.

(4) In matters, other than a challenge or the finding or sentence, the presiding officer shall have a casting vote.

133. General rule as to evidence.—The Indian Evidence Act, 1872 (1 of 1872), shall, subject to the provisions of this Act, apply to all proceedings before a court-martial.

134. Judicial notice.—A court-martial may take judicial notice of any matter within the general military knowledge of the members.

135. Summoning witnesses.—(1) The convening officer, the presiding officer of a court-martial, [1][or courts of inquiry], the judge-advocate or the commanding officer of the accused person may, by summons under his hand, require the attendance, at a time and place to be mentioned in the summons, of any person either to give evidence or to produce any document or other thing.

1. Ins. by Act 37 of 1992 , sec. 12 (w.e.f. 6-9-1992).

(2) In the case of witness amenable to military authority, the summons shall be sent to his commanding officer, and such officer shall serve it upon him accordingly.

(3) In the case of any other witness, the summons shall be sent to the magistrate within whose jurisdiction he may be or reside, and such magistrate shall give effect to the summons as if the witness were required in the court of such magistrate.

(4) When a witness is required to produce any particular document or other thing in his possession or power, the summons shall describe it with reasonable precision.

136. Documents exempted from production.—(1) Nothing in section 135 shall be deemed to affect the operation of sections 123 and 124 of the Indian Evidence Act, 1872, (1 of 1872), or to apply to any letter, postcard, telegram or other document in the custody of the postal or telegraph authorities.

(2) If any document in such custody is, in the opinion of any district magistrate, chief presidency magistrate, High Court or Court of Session, wanted for the purpose of any court-martial, such magistrate or court may require the postal or telegraph authorities, as the case may be, to deliver such document to such person as such magistrate or court may direct.

(3) If any such document is, in the opinion of any other magistrate or of any commissioner of police or district superintendent of police, wanted for any such purpose, he may require the postal or telegraph authorities, as the case may be, to cause search to be made for and to detain such document pending the orders of any such district magistrate, chief presidency magistrate or High Court or Court of Session.

137. Commissions for examination of witnesses.—(1) Whenever, in the course of a trial by court-martial, it appears to the court that the examination of a witness is necessary for the ends of justice, and that the attendance of such witness cannot be procured without an amount of delay, expense or inconvenience which, in the circumstances of the case, would be unreasonable, such court may address the Judge-Advocate General in order that a commission to take the evidence of such witness may be issued.

(2) The Judge-Advocate General may then, if he thinks necessary, issue a commission to any district magistrate or magistrate of the first class, within the local limits of whose

jurisdiction such witness resides, to take the evidence of such witness.

(3) The magistrate or officer to whom the commission is issued, or, if he is the district magistrate, he or such magistrate of the first class as he appoints in this behalf, shall proceed to the place where the witness is or shall summon the witness before him and shall take down his evidence in the same manner, and may for this purpose exercise the same powers, as in trials of warrant-cases under the [1][Code of Criminal Procedure, 1973 (2 of 1974)], or any corresponding law in force in [2][the State of Jammu and Kashmir].

(4) When the witness resides in a tribal area or in any place outside India, the commission may be issued in the manner specified in [3][Chapter XXII of the Code of Criminal Procedure, 1973 (2 of 1974)], or of any corresponding law in force in [2][the State of Jammu and Kashmir].

(5) In this and the next succeeding section, the expression "Judge-Advocate General" includes a Deputy Judge-Advocate General.

138. Examination of a witness on commission.—(1) The prosecutor and the accused person in any case in which a commission is issued under section 137 may respectively forward any interrogatories in writing which the court may think relevant to the issue, and the magistrate or officer executing the commission shall examine the witness upon such interrogatories.

(2) The prosecutor and the accused person may appear before such magistrate or officer by counsel or, except in the case of an accused person in custody, in person, and may examine, cross-examine and re-examine, as the case may be, the said witness.

(3) After a commission issued under section 137 has been duly executed, it shall be returned, together with the deposition of the witness examined thereunder, to the Judge-Advocate General.

---

1. Subs. by Act 37 of 1992, sec. 13, for "Code of Criminal Procedure, 1898 (5 of 1898)" (w.e.f. 6-9-1992).
2. Subs. by the Adaptation of Laws (No. 3) Order, 1956, for "a Part B State".
3. Subs. by Act 37 of 1992, sec. 13, for "Chapter XL of the Code of Criminal Procedure, 1898 (5 of 1898)," (w.e.f. 6-9-1992).

(4) On receipt of a commission and deposition returned under sub-section (3), the Judge-Advocate General shall forward the same to the court at whose instance the commission was issued or, if such court has been dissolved, to any other court convened for the trial of the accused person; and the commission, the return thereto and the deposition shall be open to inspection by the prosecutor and the accused person, and may, subject to all just exceptions, be read in evidence in the case by either the prosecutor or the accused, and shall form part of the proceedings of the court.

(5) In every case in which a commission is issued under section 137, the trial may be adjourned for a specified time reasonably sufficient for the execution and return of the commission.

139. Conviction of offence not charged.—(1) A person charged before a court-martial with desertion may be found guilty of attempting to desert or of being absent without leave.

(2) A person charged before a court-martial with attempting to desert may be found guilty of being absent without leave.

(3) A person charged before a court-martial with using criminal force may be found guilty of assault.

(4) A person charged before a court-martial with using threatening language may be found guilty of using insubordinate language.

(5) A person charged before a court-martial with any one of the offences specified in clauses (a), (b), (c) and (d) of section 52 may be found guilty of any other of these offences with which he might have been charged.

(6) A person charged before a court-martial with an offence punishable under section 69 may be found guilty of any other offence of which he might have been found guilty if the provisions of the [1][Code of Criminal Procedure, 1973 (2 of 1974)] were applicable.

(7) A person charged before a court-martial with any offence under this Act, may, on failure of proof of an offence having been committed in circumstances involving a more severe punishment, be found guilty of the same offence as having been committed in circumstances involving a less severe punishment.

---

1. Subs. by Act 37 of 1992, sec. 14, for "Code of Criminal Procedure, 1898 (5 of 1898)" (w.e.f. 6-9-1992).

(8) A person charged before a court-martial with any offence under this Act may be found guilty of having attempted or abetted the commission of that offence, although the attempt or abetment is not separately charged.

140. Presumption as to signatures.—In any proceeding under this Act, any application, certificate, warrant, reply or other document purporting to be signed by an officer in the service of the Government shall, on production, be presumed to have been duly signed by the person by whom and in the character in which it purports to have been signed, until the contrary is shown.

141. Enrolment paper.—(1) Any enrolment paper purporting to be signed by an enrolling officer shall, in proceedings under this Act, be evidence of the person enrolled having given the answers to questions which he is therein represented as having given.

(2) The enrolment of such person may be proved by the production of the original or a copy of his enrolment paper purporting to be certified to be a true copy by the officer having the custody of the enrolment paper.

142. Presumption as to certain documents.—(1) A letter, return or other document respecting the service of any person, or the cashiering, dismissal or discharge of any person from, any portion of the regular Army, or respecting the circumstance of any person not having served in, or belonged to, any portion of the forces, if purporting to be signed by or on behalf of the Central Government or [1][the Chief of the Army Staff], or by any prescribed officer, shall be evidence of the facts stated in such letter, return or other document.

(2) An Army, Navy or Air Force List of Gazette purporting to be published by authority shall be evidence of the status and rank of the officers, junior commissioned officers or warrant officers therein mentioned and of any appointment held by them and of the corps, battalion or arm or branch of the services to which they belong.

(3) Where a record is made in any regimental book in pursuance of this Act or of any rules made thereunder or otherwise in pursuance of military duty, and purports to be signed by the commanding officer or by the officer whose duty it is

---

1. Subs. by Act 19 of 1955, sec. 2 and Sch., for "the Commander-in-Chief".

to make such record, such record shall be evidence of the facts therein stated.

(4) A copy of any record in any regimental book purporting to be certified to be a true copy by the officer having custody of such book shall be evidence of such record.

(5) Where any person subject to this Act is being tried on a charge of desertion or of absence without leave, and such person has surrendered himself into the custody of any officer or other person subject to this Act, or any portion of the regular Army, or has been apprehended by such officer or person, a certificate purporting to be signed by such officer, or by the commanding officer of that portion of the regular Army, or by the commanding officer of the corps, department or detachment to which such person belongs, as the case may be, and stating the fact, date and place of such surrender or apprehension, and the manner in which he was dressed, shall be evidence of the matters so stated.

(6) Where any person subject to this Act is being tried on a charge of desertion or of absence without leave, and such person has surrendered himself into the custody of, or has been apprehended by, a police officer not below the rank of an officer-in-charge of a police station, a certificate purporting to be signed by such police officer and stating the fact, date and place of such surrender or apprehension and the manner in which he was dressed shall be evidence of the matters so stated.

(7) Any document purporting to be a report under the hand of any Chemical Examiner or Assistant Chemical Examiner to Government [1][or any of the Government scientific experts, namely, the Chief Inspector of the Explosives, the Director of Finger Print Bureau, the Director, Haffkeine Institute, Bombay, the Director of a Central Forensic Science Laboratory or a State Forensic Science Laboratory and the Serologist to the Government] upon any matter or thing duly submitted to him for examination or analysis and report may be used as evidence in any proceeding under this Act.

143. Reference by accused to Government officer.—(1) If at any trial for desertion or absence without leave, overstaying leave or not rejoining when warned for service, the person tried states in his defence any sufficient or reasonable excuse for his

1. Ins. by Act 37 of 1992, sec. 15 (w.e.f. 6-9-1992).

unauthorised absence, and refers in support thereof to any officer in the service of the Government or if it appears that any such officer is likely to prove or disprove the said statement in the defence, the court shall address such officer and adjourn the proceedings until his reply is received.

(2) The written reply of any officer so referred to shall, if signed by him be received in evidence and have the time effect as if made on oath before the court.

(3) If the court is dissolved before the receipt of such reply, or if the court omits to comply with the provisions of this section, the convening officer may, at his discretion, annul the proceedings and order a fresh trial.

144. Evidence of previous convictions and general character.—(1) When any person subject to this Act has been convicted by a court-martial of any offence, such court-martial may inquire into, and receive and record evidence of any previous convictions of such person, either by a court-martial or by a criminal court, or any previous award of punishment under any of the sections 80, 83, 84 and 85 and may further inquire into and record the general character of such person and such other matters as may be prescribed.

(2) Evidence received under this section may be either oral, or in the shape of entries in, or certified extracts from, court-martial books or other official records; and it shall not be necessary to give notice before trial to the person tried that evidence as to his previous convictions or character will be received.

(3) At a summary court-martial the officer holding the trial may, if he thinks fit, record any previous convictions against the offender, his general character, and such other matters as may be prescribed, as of his own knowledge, instead of requiring them to be proved under the foregoing provisions of this section.

145. Lunacy of accused.—(1) Whenever, in the course of a trial by court-martial, it appears to the court that the person charged is by reason of unsoundness of mind incapable of making his defence, or that he committed that act alleged but was by reason of unsoundness of mind incapable of knowing the nature of the act of knowing that it was wrong or contrary to law, the court shall record a finding accordingly.

The presiding officer of the court, or, in the case of a summary court-martial, the officer holding the trial, shall forthwith report the case to the confirming officer, or to the authority empowered to deal with its finding under section 162, as the case may be.

(2) The confirming officer to whom the case is reported under sub-section (2) may, if he does not confirm the finding, take steps to have the accused person tried by the same or another court-martial for the offence with which he was charged.

(3) The authority to whom the finding of a summary court-martial is reported under sub-section (2), and a confirming officer confirming a finding in any case so reported to him shall order the accused person to be kept in custody in the prescribed manner and shall report the case for the orders of the Central Government.

(4) On receipt of a report under sub-section (4) the Central Government may order the accused person to be detained in a lunatic asylum or other suitable place of safe custody.

146. Subsequent fitness of lunatic accused for trial.—Where any accused person, having been found by reason of unsoundness of mind to be incapable of making his defence, is in custody or under detention under section 145, the officer commanding the army, army corps, division or brigade within the area of whose command the accused is in custody or is detained, or any other officer prescribed in this behalf, may—

(a) if such person is in custody under sub-section (4) of section 145, on the report of a medical officer that he is capable of making his defence; or

(b) if such person is detained in a jail under sub-section (5) of section 145, on a certificate of the Inspector General of Prisons, and if such person is detained in a lunatic asylum under the said sub-section on a certificate of any two or more of the visitors of such asylum that he is capable of making his defence,

take steps to have such person tried by the same or another court-martial for the offence with which he was originally charged or, if the offence is a civil offence, by criminal court.

147. Transmission to Central Government of orders under section 146.—A copy of every order made by an officer under section 146 for the trial of the accused shall forthwith be sent to the Central Government.

148. Release of lunatic accused.—Where any person is in custody under sub-section (4) of section 145 or under detention under sub-section (5) of that section—

(a) if such person is in custody under the said sub-section (4), on the report of a medical officer, or

(b) if such person is detained under the said sub-section (5), on a certificate from any of the authorities mentioned in clause (b) of section 146 that, in the judgment of such officer or authority such person may be released without danger of his doing injury to himself or to any other person,

the Central Government may order that such person be released or detained in custody, or transferred to a public lunatic asylum if he has not already been sent to such an asylum.

149. Delivery of lunatic accused to relatives.—Where any relative or friend of any person who is in custody under sub-section (4) of section 145 or under detention under sub-section (5) of that section desires that he should be delivered to his care and custody, the Central Government may upon application by such relative or friend and on his giving security to the satisfaction of that government that the person delivered shall be properly taken care of and prevented from doing injury to himself or any other person, and be produced for the inspection of such officer, and at such times and places, as the Central Government may direct, order such person to be delivered to such relative or friend.

150. Order for custody and disposal of property pending trial.—When any property regarding which any offence appears to have been committed, or which appears to have been used for the commission of any offence, is produced before a court-martial during a trial, the court may make such order as it thinks fit for the proper custody of such property pending the conclusion of the trial, and if the property is subject to speedy or natural decay may, after recording such evidence as it thinks necessary, order it to be sold or otherwise disposed of.

151. Order for disposal of property regarding which offence is committed.—(1) After the conclusion of trial before any court-martial the court or the officer confirming the finding or sentence of such court-martial, or any authority superior to such officer, or, in the case of a court-martial whose finding or sentence does not require confirmation, the officer commanding the army, army corps, division or brigade within which the trial was held, may make such order as it or he thinks fit for the disposal by destruction, confiscation, delivery to any person claiming to be entitled to possession thereof, or otherwise, of any property or document produced before the court or in its custody, or regarding which any offence appears to have been committed or which has been used for the commission of any offence.

(2) Where any order has been made under sub-section (1) in respect of property regarding which an offence appears to have been committed, a copy of such order signed and certified by the authority making the same may, whether the trial was held within India or not, be sent to a magistrate within whose jurisdiction such property for the time being is situated and such magistrate shall thereupon cause the order to be carried into effect as if it were an order passed by him under the provisions of the [1][Code of Criminal Procedure, 1973 (2 of 1974)], or any corresponding law in force in [2][the State of Jammu and Kashmir].

(3) In this section the term "property" includes in the case of property regarding which an offence appears to have been committed, not only such property as has been originally in the possession or under the control of any person, but also any property into or for which the same may have been converted or exchanged, and any thing acquired by such conversion or exchange whether immediately or otherwise.

152. Powers of court-martial in relation to proceedings under this Act.—Any trial by a court-martial under the provisions of this Act shall be deemed to be a judicial proceeding within the meaning of sections 193 and 228 of the Indian Penal Code (45 of 1860) and the court-martial shall be deemed to be a court within the meaning of [3][sections 345 and 346 of the Code of Criminal Procedure, 1973 (2 of 1974)].

1. Subs. by Act 37 of 1992, sec. 14, for "Code of Criminal Procedure, 1898 (5 of 1898)" (w.e.f. 6-9-1992).
2. Subs. by the Adaptation of Laws (No. 3) Order, 1956, for "a Part B State".
3. Subs. by Act 37 of 1992, sec. 16, for "section 480 and 482 of the Code of Criminal Procedure, 1898 (5 of 1898)" (w.e.f. 6-9-1992).

CHAPTER XII

CONFIRMATION AND REVISION

153. Finding and sentence not valid, unless confirmed.—No finding or sentence of a general, district or summary general, court-martial shall be valid except so far as it may be confirmed as provided by this Act.

COMMENTS

Findings and sentence rendered by General Court-Martial and confirmed by the Chief of Army Staff are not liable to be interfered with; *Union of India* v. *J.S. Brar*, AIR 1993 SC 773.

154. Power to confirm finding and sentence of general court-martial.—The findings and sentences of general courts-martial may be confirmed by the Central Government, or by any officer empowered in this behalf by warrant of the Central Government.

155. Power to confirm finding and sentence of district court-martial.—The findings and sentences of district courts-martial may be confirmed by any officer having power to convene a general court-martial or by any officer empowered in this behalf by warrant of such officer.

156. Limitation of powers of confirming authority.—A warrant issued under section 154 or section 155 may contain such restrictions, reservations or conditions as the authority issuing it may think fit.

157. Power to confirm finding and sentence of summary general court-martial.—The findings and sentences of summary general courts-martial may be confirmed by the convening officer or if he so directs, by an authority superior to him.

158. Power of confirming authority to mitigate, remit or commute sentences.—(1) Subject to such restrictions, reservations or conditions as may be contained in any warrant issued under section 154 or section 155 and to the provision of sub-section (2), a confirming authority may, when confirming the sentence of a court-martial, mitigate or remit the punishment thereby awarded, or commute that punishment for any punishment or punishments lower in the scale laid down in section 71.

(2) A sentence of transportation shall not be commuted for a sentence of imprisonment for a term exceeding the term of transportation awarded by the court.*

159. Confirming of findings and sentences on board a ship.—When any person subject to this Act is tried and sentenced by a court-martial while on board a ship, the finding and sentence so far as not confirmed and executed on board the ship, may be confirmed and executed in like manner as if such person had been tried at the port of disembarkation.

160. Revision of finding or sentence.—(1) Any finding or sentence of a court-martial which requires confirmation may be once revised by order of the confirming authority and on such revision, the court, if so directed by the confirming authority, may take additional evidence.

(2) The court, on revision, shall consist of the same officers as were present when the original decision was passed, unless any of those officers are unavoidably absent.

(4) In case of such unavoidable absence the cause thereof shall be duly certified in the proceedings, and the court shall proceed with the revision, provided that, if a general court-martial, it still consists of five officers, or, if a summary general or district court-martial, of three officers.

161. Finding and sentence of a summary court-martial.—(1) Save as otherwise provided in sub-section (2), the finding and sentence of a summary court-martial shall not require to be confirmed, but may be carried out forthwith.

(2) If the officer holding the trial is of less than five years service, he shall not, except on active service, carry into effect any sentence until it has received the approval of an officer commanding not less than a brigade.

162. Transmission of proceedings of summary courts-martial.—The proceedings of every summary court-martial shall without delay be forwarded to the officer commanding the division or brigade within which the trial was held, or to the prescribed officer; and such officer, or [1][the Chief of the Army

---

* *See* section 53A of the Indian Penal Code (45 of 1860).

1. Subs. by Act 19 of 1955, sec. 2 and Sch., for "the Commander-in-Chief".

Staff], or any officer empowered in this behalf by [1][the Chief of the Army Staff], may, for reasons based on the merits of the case, but not any merely technical grounds, set-aside the proceedings or reduce the sentence to any other sentence which the court might have passed.

163. Alteration of finding or sentence in certain cases.—(1) Where a finding of guilty by a court-martial, which has been confirmed, or which does not require confirmation, is found for any reason to be invalid or cannot be supported by the evidence, the authority which would have had power under section 179 to commute the punishment awarded by the sentence, if the finding had been valid, may substitute a new finding and pass a sentence for the offence specified or involved in such finding:

Provided that no such substitution shall be made unless such finding could have been validly made by the court-martial on the charge and unless it appears that the court-martial must have been satisfied of the facts establishing the said offence.

(2) Where a sentence passed by a court-martial which has been confirmed, or which does not require confirmation, not being a sentence passed in pursuance of a new finding substituted under sub-section (1), is found for any reason to be invalid, the authority referred to in sub-section (1) may pass a valid sentence.

(3) The punishment awarded by a sentence passed under sub-section (1) or sub-section (2) shall not be higher in the scale of punishments than, or in excess of, the punishment awarded by, the sentence for which a new sentence is substituted under this section.

(4) Any finding substituted, or any sentence passed, under this section shall, for the purposes of this Act and the rules made thereunder, have effect as if it were a finding or sentence, as the case may be, of a court-martial.

164. Remedy against order, finding or sentence of court-martial.—(1) Any person subject to this Act who considers himself aggrieved by any order passed by any court-martial may present a petition to the officer or authority empowered to confirm any finding or sentence of such court-martial, and the confirming

1. Subs. by Act 19 of 1955, sec. 2 and Sch., for "the Commander-in-Chief".

authority may take such steps as may be considered necessary to satisfy itself as to the correctness, legality or propriety of the order passed or as to the regularity of any proceeding to which the order relates.

(2) Any person subject to this Act who considers himself aggrieved by a finding or sentence of any court-martial which has been confirmed, may present a petition to the Central Government, [1][the Chief of the Army Staff] or any prescribed officer superior in command to the one who confirmed such finding or sentence, and the Central Government, [1][the Chief of the Army Staff] or other officer, as the case may be, may pass such orders thereon as it or he thinks fit.

COMMENTS

Reasons are not required to be recorded for an order passed by the confirming authority confirming the findings and sentence by the court-martial as well as the order passed by the Central Government dismissing the post-confirmation petition; *S.N. Mukherjee* v. *Union of India,* AIR 1990 SC 1984.

165. Annulment of proceedings.—The Central Government, [1][the Chief of the Army Staff] or any prescribed officer may annul the proceedings of any court-martial on the ground that they are illegal or unjust.

CHAPTER XIII

EXECUTION OF SENTENCES

166. Form of sentence of death.—In awarding a sentence of death a court-martial shall, in its discretion, direct that the offender shall suffer death by being hanged by the neck until he be dead, or shall suffer death by being shot to dead.

167. Commencement of sentence of transportation or imprisonment.—Whenever any person is sentenced by a court-martial under this Act to transportation or imprisonment, the term of his sentence shall, whether it has been revised or not, be reckoned to commence on the day on which the original proceedings were signed by the presiding officer or, in the case of a summary court-martial, by the court.

1. Subs. by Act 19 of 1955, sec. 2 and Sch., for "the Commander-in-Chief".

168. Execution of sentence of transportation.—Whenever any sentence of transportation is passed under this Act or whenever any sentence of death is commuted to transportation, the commanding officer of the person under sentence or such other officer as may be prescribed shall forward a warrant in the prescribed form to the officer in charge of the civil prison in which such person is to be confined and shall arrange for his despatch to such prison with the warrant.

169. Execution of sentence of imprisonment.—(1) Whenever any sentence of imprisonment is passed under this Act by a court-martial or whenever any sentence of death of transportation is commuted to imprisonment, the confirming officer or in case of a summary court-martial, the officer holding the court or such other officer as may be prescribed, shall, save as otherwise provided in sub-sections (3) and (4), direct either that the sentence shall be carried out by confinement in a military prison or that it shall be carried out by confinement in a civil prison.

(2) When a direction has been made under sub-section (1), the commanding officer, of the person under sentence or such other officer as may be prescribed shall forward a warrant in the prescribed form to the officer incharge of the prison in which such person is to be confined and shall arrange for his despatch to such prison with the warrant.

(3) In the case of a sentence of imprisonment for a period not exceeding three months and passed under this Act by a court-martial, the appropriate officer under sub-section (1), may direct that the sentence shall be carried out by confinement in military custody instead of in a civil or military prison.

(4) On active service, a sentence of imprisonment may be carried out by confinement in such place as the officer commanding the forces in the field may from time-to-time, appoint.

[1][**169A. Period of custody undergone by the officer or person to be set off against the imprisonment.**—When a person or officer subject to this Act is sentenced by a court-martial to a term of imprisonment, not being an imprisonment in default of payment of fine, the period spent by him in civil or military custody during investigation, inquiry or trial of the same case, and before the date

1. Ins. by Act 37 of 1992, sec. 17 (w.e.f. 6-9-1992).

of order of such sentence, shall be set off against the term of imprisonment imposed upon him, and the liability of such person or officer to undergo imprisonment on such order of sentence shall be restricted to the remainder, if any, of the term of imprisonment imposed upon him.]

170. Temporary custody of offender.—Where a sentence of transportation or imprisonment is directed to be undergone in a civil prison the offender may be kept in a military prison or in military custody or in any other fit place, till such time as it is possible to send him to a civil prison.

171. Execution of sentence of imprisonment in special cases.—Whenever, in the opinion of an officer commanding an army, army corps, division or independent brigade, any sentence or portion of a sentence of imprisonment, cannot for special reasons, conveniently be carried out in a military prison or in military custody in accordance with the provisions of section 169 such officer may direct that such sentence or portion of sentence shall be carried out by confinement in any civil prison or other fit place.

172. Conveyance of prisoner from place to place.—A person under sentence of transportation or imprisonment may, during this conveyance from place to place, or when on board ship, aircraft, or otherwise, be subjected to such restraint as is necessary for his safe conduct and removal.

173. Communication of certain orders to prison officers.—Whenever an order is duly made under this Act setting-aside or varying any sentence, order or warrant under which any person is confined in a civil or military prison, a warrant in accordance with such order shall be forwarded by the officer making the order or his staff officer or such other person as may be prescribed to the officer in charge of the prison in which such person is confined.

174. Execution of sentence of fine.—When a sentence of fine is imposed by a court-martial under section 69 whether the trial was held within India or not, a copy of such sentence, signed and certified by the confirming officer, or where no confirmation is required, by the officer holding the trial may be sent to any magistrate in India, and such magistrate shall thereupon cause the fine to be recovered in accordance with the provisions of the

[1][Code of Criminal Procedure, 1973 (2 of 1974)] or any corresponding law in force in [2][the State of Jammu and Kashmir] for the levy of fines as if it were a sentence of fine imposed by such magistrate.

175. Establishment and regulation of military prisons.—The Central Government may set apart any building or part of a building, or any place under its control, as a military prison for the confinement of persons sentenced to imprisonment under this Act.

176. Informality or error in the order or warrant.—Whenever any person is sentenced to transportation or imprisonment under this Act, and is undergoing the sentence in any place or manner in which he might be confined under a lawful order or warrant in pursuance of this Act, the confinement of such person shall not be deemed to be illegal only by reason of any informality or error in or as respects the order, warrant or other document, or the authority by which, or in pursuance whereof such person was brought into or is confined in any such place, and any such order, warrant or document may be amended accordingly.

177. Power to make rules in respect of prisons and prisoners.—The Central Government may make rules providing—

(a) for the government, management and regulation of military prisons;

(b) for the appointment, removal and powers of inspectors, visitors, governors and officers thereof;

(c) for the labour of prisoners undergoing confinement therein, and for enabling persons to earn, by special industry and good conduct, a remission of a portion of their sentence;

(d) for the safe custody of prisoners and the maintenance of discipline among them and the punishment, by personal correction, restraint or otherwise, of offences committed by prisoners;

(e) for the application to military prisons of any of the provisions of the Prisons Act, 1894 (9 of 1894), relating to

1. Subs. by Act 37 of 1992, sec. 14, for "Code of Criminal Procedure 1898 (5 of 1898)" (w.e.f. 6-9-1992).
2. Subs. by the Adaptation of Laws (No. 3) Order, 1956, for "a Part B State".

the duties of officers of prisons and the punishment of persons not being prisoners;

(f) for the admission into any prison, at proper times and subject to proper restrictions, of persons with whom prisoners may desire to communicate, and for the consultation by prisoners under trial with their legal advisers without the presence as far as possible of any third party within hearing distance.

178. Restriction of rule-making power in regard to corporal punishment.—Rules made under section 177 shall not authorise corporal punishment to be inflicted for any offence, nor render the imprisonment more severe than it is under the law for the time being in force relating to civil prisons.

CHAPTER XIV

PARDONS, REMISSIONS AND SUSPENSIONS

179. Pardon and remission.—When any person subject to this Act has been convicted by a court-martial of any offence, the Central Government or [1][the Chief of the Army Staff] or, in the case of a sentence, which he could have confirmed or which did not require confirmation, the officer commanding the army, army corps, division or independent brigade in which such person at the time of conviction was serving, or the prescribed officer may—

(a) either with or without conditions which the person sentenced accepts, pardon the person or remit the whole or any part of the punishment awarded; or

(b) mitigate the punishment awarded; or

(c) commute such punishment for any less punishment or punishments mentioned in this Act:

Provided that a sentence of transportation* shall not be commuted for a sentence of imprisonment for a term exceeding the term of transportation awarded by the court; or

(d) either with or without conditions which the person sentenced accepts, release the person on parole.

---

1. Subs. by Act 19 of 1955, sec. 2 and Sch., for "the Commander-in-Chief".

* *See* section 53A of the Indian Penal Code (45 of 1860).

180. Cancellation of conditional pardon, release on parole or remission.—(1) If any condition on which a person has been pardoned or released on parole or a punishment has been remitted is, in the opinion of the authority which granted the pardon, release or remission, not fulfilled, such authority may cancel the pardon, release or remission, and thereupon the sentence of the court shall be carried into effect as if such pardon, release or remission had not been granted.

(2) A person whose sentence of transportation* or imprisonment is carried into effect under the provisions of sub-section (1) shall undergo only the unexpired portion of his sentence.

181. Reduction of warrant officer or non-commissioned officer.—When under the provisions of section 77, a warrant officer or a non-commissioned officer is deemed to be reduced to the ranks, such reduction shall, for the purpose of section 179, be treated as a punishment awarded by a sentence of a court-martial.

182. Suspension of sentence of transportation* or imprisonment.—(1) Where a person subject to this Act is sentenced by a court-martial to transportation or imprisonment, the Central Government, [1][the Chief of the Army Staff] or any officer empowered to convene a general or a summary general court-martial, may suspend the sentence whether or not the offender has already been committed to prison or to military custody.

(2) The authority or officer specified in sub-section (1) may, in the case of an offender so sentenced direct that, until the orders of such authority or officer have been obtained the offender shall not be committed to prison or to military custody.

(3) The powers conferred by sub-sections (1) and (2) may be exercised in the case of any such sentence which has been confirmed, reduced or commuted.

183. Orders pending suspension.—(1) Where the sentence referred to in section 182 is imposed by a court-martial other than a summary court-martial, the confirming officer may, when

---

* *See* section 53A of the Indian Penal Code (45 of 1860).

1. Subs. by Act 19 of 1955, sec. 2 and Sch., for "the Commander-in-Chief".

confirming the sentence, direct that the offender be not committed to prison or to military custody until the orders of the authority or officer specified in section 182 have been obtained.

(2) Where a sentence of imprisonment is imposed by a summary court-martial, the officer holding the trial or the officer authorised to approve of the sentence under sub-section (2) of section 161, may make the direction referred to in sub-section (1).

184. Release on suspension.—Where a sentence is suspended under section 182, the offender shall forthwith be released from custody.

185. Computation of period of suspension.—Any period during which the sentence is under suspension shall be reckoned as part of the term of such sentence.

186. Order after suspension.—The authority or officer specified in section 182 may, at any time while a sentence is suspended, order—

(a) that the offender be committed to undergo the unexpired portion of the sentence, or

(b) that the sentence be remitted.

187. Reconsideration of case after suspension.—(1) Where a sentence has been suspended, the case may at any time, and shall at intervals of not more than four months, be reconsidered by the authority or officer specified in section 182, or by any general or other officer not below the rank of field officer duly authorised by the authority or officer specified in section 182.

(2) Where on such reconsideration by the officer so authorised it appears to him that the conduct of the offender since his conviction has been such as to justify a remission of the sentence, he shall refer the matter to the authority or officer specified in section 182.

188. Fresh sentence after suspension.—Where an offender, while a sentence on him is suspended under this Act, is sentenced for any other offence, then—

(a) if the further sentence is also suspended under this Act, the two sentences shall run concurrently;

(b) if the further sentence is for a period of three months or more and is not suspended under this Act, the offender shall also be committed to prison or military custody for the unexpired portion of the previous sentence, but both sentences shall run concurrently; and

(c) if the further sentence is for a period of less than three months and is not suspended under this Act, the offender shall be so committed on that sentence only, and the previous sentence shall, subject to any order which may be passed under section 186 or section 187, continue to be suspended.

189. Scope of power of suspension.—The powers conferred by sections 182 and 186 shall be in addition to and not in derogation of the power of mitigation, remission and commutation.

190. Effect of suspension and remission on dismissal.—(1) Where in addition to any other sentence the punishment of dismissal has been awarded by a court-martial, and such other sentence is suspended under section 182, then, such dismissal shall not take effect until so ordered by the authority or officer specified in section 182.

(2) If such other sentence is remitted under section 186, the punishment of dismissal shall also be remitted.

CHAPTER XV

RULES

191. Power to make rules.—(1) The Central Government may make rules[1] for the purpose of carrying into effect the provisions of this Act.

(2) Without prejudice to the generality of the power conferred by sub-section (1), the rules made thereunder may provide for—

(a) the removal, retirement, release or discharge from the service of persons subject to this Act;

(b) the amount and incidence of fines to be imposed under section 89;

[2][***]

(d) the assembly and procedure of courts of inquiry, the recording of summaries of evidence and the administration of oaths or affirmations by such courts;

---

1. *See* Army Rules, 1954, published in the Gazette of India, 1954, Pt. II, Sec. 4, p. 291.

2. Clause (c) omitted by Act 37 of 1992, sec. 13 (w.e.f. 6-9-1992).

(e) the convening and constituting of courts-martial and the appointment of prosecutors at trials by courts-martial;

(f) the adjournment, dissolution and sitting of courts-martial;

(g) the procedure to be observed in trials by courts-martial and the appearance of legal practitioners thereat;

(h) the confirmation, revision and annulment of, and petitions against, the findings and sentences of courts-martial;

(i) the carrying into effect of sentences of courts-martial;

(j) the forms of orders to be made under the provisions of this Act relating to courts-martial, transportation and imprisonment;

(k) the constitution of authorities to decide for what persons, to what amounts and in what manner, provision should be made for dependants under section 99, and the due carrying out of such decisions;

(l) the relative rank of the officers, junior commissioned officers, warrant officers, petty officers, and non-commissioned officers of the regular Army, Navy and Air Force when acting together;

(m) any other matter directed by this Act to be prescribed.

192. Power to make regulations.—The Central Government may make regulations for all or any of the purposes of this Act other than those specified in section 191.

COMMENTS

Pension Regulations for the Army made under section 192 of the Act do not provide for automatic forfeiture of pension or gratuity. The cases of voluntary resignations of officers, who have to their credit the minimum period of qualifying service are not covered by Regulations 3 and 16 and, therefore, such officers, who voluntary resign, cannot be automatically deprived of the terminal benefits; *Union of India* v. *Lt. Col. P.S. Bhargava*, AIR 1997 SC 565.

193. Publication of rules and regulations in Gazette.—All rules and regulations made under this Act shall be published in the Official Gazette and, on such publication, shall have effect as if enacted in this Act.

[1][**193A. Rules and regulations to be laid before Parliament.**—Every rule and every regulation made by the Central Government under this Act shall be laid, as soon as may be after it is made, before each House of Parliament while it is in session, for a total period of thirty days which may be comprised in one session or in two or more successive sessions, and if, before the expiry of the session immediately following the session, or the successive sessions aforesaid, both Houses agree in making any modification in the rule or regulation or both Houses agree that the rule or regulation should not be made, the rule or regulation shall thereafter have effect only in such modified form or be of no effect, as the case may be; so, however, that any such modification or annulment shall be without prejudice to the validity of anything previously done under that rule or regulation.]

194. Repeals.—[*Rep. by the Repealing and Amending Act, 1957 (36 of 1957), sec. 2 and Sch. I. (w.e.f. 17-9-1957).*]

[2][***]

Chapter XVI

[*Repealed*]

195. Definition of "British Officer".—[*Rep. by the Army (Amendment) Act, 1992 (37 of 1992), sec. 19 (w.e.f. 6-9-1992).*]

196. Power of British Officer.—[*Rep. by the Army (Amendment) Act, 1992 (37 of 1992), sec. 19 (w.e.f. 6-9-1992).*]

THE SCHEDULE.—[*Rep. by the Repealing and Amending Act, 1957 (36 of 1957), sec. 2 and Sch. I. (w.e.f. 17-9-1957).*]

---

1. Ins. by Act 20 of 1983, sec. 2 and Sch. (w.e.f. 15-3-1984).
2. Chapter XVI and the heading "TRANSITORY PROVISIONS" omitted by Act 37 of 1992, sec. 19 (w.e.f. 6-9-1992).

May I request you to kindly change the statue with that of a male. My client fears that it may favour his wife during the trial for cruelty and maintenance.

HURRY

PURCHASE ONE NUKE BOMB, GET 1100 AK-47, 3 LAKH GRANADES, 5 LAKH LIVE ROUNDS..... ABSOLUTELY FREE, OFFER VALID TILL BORDER PROBLEM IS SOLVED

FOR DETAILS, CONTACT, HIDE OUT NO. ?? NEAR LOC

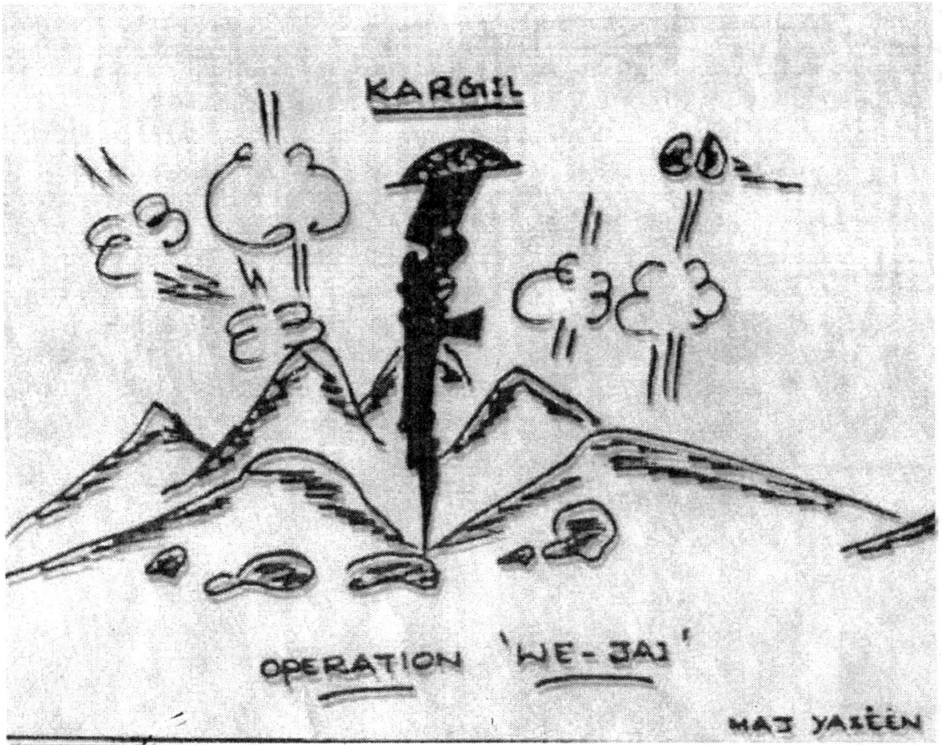
KARGIL
OPERATION 'WE-JAJ'
MAJ YASEEN

Yes Madam! You have been cheated by your husband on your birthday. It is not American Chiffon, but a local saree costing not more than Rs. 175/- only.

Oh! That pretty woman is on leave for six months, No problem.
I will come after six months. I want these pension papers get processed urgently.

No! The guy with Jersy No. 99 wants a bottle of Wisky,
That's why he is showing "W" Sign, instead of victory sign.

JUSTICE DE-'LIED'
IS
JUSTICE DE-'KNIFED'

I swear by 'Solan' No.-1, that what I shall be the 'small' of truth, the label of whole truth and "Patiala" of nothing but the truth.

The legal awareness and due adherence to the existing legal provisions has come to acquire increasing importance for the commanders at all levels. Staff Officers posted to 'A' branch are expected to correctly apply the latest rulings on the cases processed by them. However, non-availability of suitable reference is a major handicap to them.

The book is an attempt to compile and catalogue the powers available to the formation commanders in connection with various aspects having legal bearings. It aims to appropriately equip them to apply their mind for fair and correct action on a wide range of cases having disciplinary and legal bearings.

The information and reference material included in this book would be of practicable use to the staff officers at various Headquarters and others concerned with the correct and timely disposal of pending cases.

Maj Gen Nilendra Kumar was the Judge Advocate General of Indian Army. An alumnus of Lucknow University and Jamna Lal Bajaj Institute of Management Studies, Mumbai, he passed out from the National Defence Academy. He was commissioned in the Regiment of Artillery and took part in Indo Pak war, 1971 on the western front. He conducted a large number of courts martial. A prolific writer on military law, he addresses issues concerning security jurisprudence, human rights, law of war and disarmament. He is presently Director Amity Law School, Amity University, UP, Noida.